mozaic

FRENCH CUISINE, BALINESE FLAVOURS

BY CHRIS SALANS

Mozaic: French Cuisine, Balinese Flavours
was made possible thanks to the generous support of:

Anything else is a compromise

MANAGING EDITOR
Francis Dorai

EDITORS
Rachael Morris
Sng Siok Ai

PRODUCTION MANAGER
Sin Kam Cheong

PUBLISHED BY
Editions Didier Millet Pte Ltd
121 Telok Ayer Street #03-01
Singapore 068590
www.edmbooks.com

COLOUR SEPARATION BY
Pica Digital Pte Ltd, Singapore

PRINTED BY
Tien Wah Press Pte Ltd

Printed in Singapore

This paperback edition published in 2014

ISBN
978-981-4610-04-9

mozaic

FRENCH CUISINE, BALINESE FLAVOURS

BY CHRIS SALANS

TEXT BY Diana Darling
PHOTOGRAPHY BY Philippe Heurtault

contents

foreword

Cooking is a universal language. The culinary philosophy Chris and I share is based on the best raw materials, perfect technique, and a *savoir-faire* guided by curiosity, intuition and sheer enthusiasm. Through our common passion, we found friendship, and we want to share not only our discoveries but also the pleasure we find in collaboration or, as I call it, "playing a piano with four hands", in complete harmony. Chris's talent is innate. He breathes life into his dishes, juggling flavours and spices to regale the gourmets of Bali and the world. I see him as the high priest of the here and now, and also of elsewhere and other times, the master at marrying Indonesian flavours with classic French cuisine and technique. He is superb at communicating his passion and making it come to glorious life, to the pleasure of all who know him. Mozaic restaurant is the epitome of the art of living and good food. One might be tempted to say that Chris practises the art of mosaic at his stoves, masterfully wielding all the ingredients necessary to tease our palates. His art astonishes, charms and enchants us. May Chris continue to travel down the road of excellence – Alsace and Bali have signed a contract for a cross-cultural marriage made in heaven.

Émile Jung
Au Crocodile, Strasbourg, France

Chris Salans has been a friend and colleague for almost a decade. We were introduced to each other through our common interest and great passion for ingredients. On that particular day, it was an interest in the black winter truffle that brought us together. We both had the fortunate experience of accompanying Pierre-Jean Pébeyre (the king of the truffle world), and Western Australian chef and my good mate Alain Fabrègues on a tour of the south Western Australian countryside to inspect truffle farms. Since that day, Chris and I have spent time in each other's company and in each other's restaurants in Indonesia and Melbourne, always passionately talking about food. Through this collection of modern recipes, I am very proud to witness the evolution of Chris's repertoire from classic French to Balinese-inspired classic fine dining – combining the best of local ingredients and French cookery techniques. What I take from this book is not only a story about a love affair with a country, but also a love affair with a chef's heritage – Chris's innate talents and the events that have led him to this time and place.

Shannon Bennett
Vue De Monde, Melbourne, Australia

mozaic
RESTAURANT
WORKSHOP
CATERING
LOUNGE
GASTRONOMIQUES
mozaic
RESTAURANT
WORKSHOP
CATERING
LOUNGE
GASTRONOMIQUES

preface

For over 15 years, Bali has been my home, my host and my inspiration. Over those years, I have admired this beautiful island and she, in turn, has provided me with a bounty of amazing ingredients that have allowed me to create Mozaic and its signature tastes. Like many of you, I have longed for this cookbook for some time and it finally gives me great pleasure to be able to share my experiences and my passion for Bali as a chef, restaurateur and resident. Bali is undeniably famous for its rich culture, generous people, and stunning beaches and surf. While these attractions have helped make her what she is to so many people today, I hope to do my part in helping put Bali and the Indonesian *terroir* on the culinary world map.

I wanted to share what Bali has given me in terms of ingredients and rich culinary culture, as it has helped me find my footing in the culinary world. Browsing the traditional markets, having family, friends and suppliers introduce me to unexpected tastes and flavours – it is through these daily discoveries that I have been able to create magic at Mozaic. Embarking on this project, though, I had no idea of the work, time and commitment involved in translating my embryonic ideas into what was to become this cookbook you now hold in your hands.

To this end, some key people have been instrumental in sharing their professional knowledge and helping to bring this book to reality, and I would like to sincerely thank them. My thanks and gratitude go to Philippe Heurtault for his beautiful images, writer Diana Darling for her evocative words and my publisher, Editions Didier Millet, and its team led by managing editor Francis Dorai.

Before you embark on this culinary adventure with me, I must thank Miele and Schott Zwiesel, who believed in this ambitious project and supported me from the outset.

I cannot go further without thanking the Mozaic team, whom I have come to regard as my second family: chef de cuisine James Ephraim, general manager Nicola Scarramuzzino, restaurant manager and sommelier Cok Senajaya and the rest of the Mozaic staff, as well as my public relations consultant Maryse LaRocque, without whom this book would never have happened.

I want to thank those closest to me: my parents, who helped make me who I am today, my lovely wife Erni and our children Nicolas and Laura. Without them, Bali may never have become my home.

I hope this book entices you to come to Bali and discover another side of the Island of the Gods. This book is my way of paying homage to the beautiful, mystical and magical island of Bali.

Bon appétit
Chris Salans

Miele
Miele
Miele
INDUCTION

ABOUT CHRIS SALANS AND MOZAIC

This is the story of a mosaic of flavours and cultures – the journey of young and gifted French-American chef Chris Salans from the rarefied *haute cuisine* centres of Europe and the United States to the great natural abundance of Indonesia, with all its mysterious scents and earthy flavours. This is the story of his discoveries and the evolution of his cuisine.

The island

Mozaic, the gastronomic restaurant founded by Chris in 2001, is situated amidst a profusion of tropical vegetation in the village of Sanggingan, Ubud, in the foothills of Bali, the fabled island that lies at the heart of the Indonesian archipelago – a vast chain of some 17,500 islands stretching between China and Australia, from the Indian Ocean to the South China Sea.

Although Indonesia is the world's third-largest democracy, it is curiously unknown to most of the world. Indeed, it rarely appears in world weather reports and is often confused in some peoples' minds with Indochina. Yet, the archipelago has long been a crossroads for trade between India, China, the Middle East and Europe, all of which had a strong cultural influence on the region. Traders came to Indonesia for the hardwoods, resins and other forest products that grew there, as well as for gold and gemstones. Most famously, they came to procure spices, a practice with tremendous geopolitical consequences that are still felt some 600 years later.

Indonesia is home to some of the oldest civilisations on earth, and traces of ancient ways of life are still apparent in its forests, villages and cultivated fields. The country's benign climate and the richness of its volcanic soils – especially in the "Asian" half of the archipelago, which includes Sumatra, Java, Bali and Borneo – have allowed its people to till the land using very rudimentary technology right up to the present day. As a result, there is still an intimacy between the people, the earth and the seas, and they have acquired a deep knowledge of the natural world.

Bali, a small island just east of Java, is better known throughout the world than the Republic of Indonesia, of which it is a province. During the 400 years of Dutch dominance in the archipelago, Bali was a somewhat neglected anomaly, a Hindu island in a region that was largely Islamic. The Dutch conquered Bali by force in 1908. Within 20 years, Bali evolved into an exotic destination for early tourists from the West, and today, the island is widely regarded as a premier centre for luxury tourism, the inland hub of which is Ubud.

Nonetheless, despite the profusion of spas, villas, smart hotels and restaurants in southern-central Bali, much of the island is still agrarian. Its fishermen still cast their nets from colourful little outrigger boats called *prahu*, virgin rainforests still cover the volcanic mountains in the centre of the island, its 1,000-year-old terraced rice fields are still worked by small farmers, and its time-honoured culture remains largely intact.

Balinese food traditions are largely based on what one finds growing on one's land, whether cultivated or wild, and in the local farmers' markets. Rice is the most esteemed staple, but much interest lies in what accompanies

PREVIOUS PAGE **The Mozaic garden at night.**
OPPOSITE **In the Workshop preparing a Chef's Table dinner.**
ABOVE **At a streetside food stall in Bali.**

FROM TOP LEFT CLOCKWISE A young boy with his catch of the day; Pura Danau Bratan, the famous Hindu temple on Bratan Lake – every village has two or three main temples, as well as agricultural and clan temples; Balinese people at communal prayer during a temple festival, with offerings in the lower left corner; Bali's famous terraced rice fields – rice is the principal agricultural crop in Bali; A fisherman casting his net on the east coast of Bali, which supports a small fish-processing industry; Balinese market scene – traditional farmers' markets are held every three days on a rotating basis among groups of villages.

FROM LEFT Chris on his first day at Le Cordon Bleu in Paris; Chris at his grandparents' house in the French countryside after a day of picking mushrooms.

it, including a wide array of intensely spiced side dishes. The most fundamental of these are a variety of chilli-based condiments called *sambal*. These are usually given extra punch with fermented shrimp paste. Vegetable dishes may be made from cultivated varieties, wild greens or very young fruit, often prepared with fresh coconut, and always with freshly ground spices. Until recently, meat was eaten mainly at ceremonial occasions, and the main source of protein for many people in Bali is still salt fish, eggs, nuts, tofu (*tahu*) and the Javanese fermented soya cakes known as tempeh. Fruit is generally eaten in a pungent salad (*rujak*) as an afternoon snack.

Spices are usually ground by hand with mortar and pestle in this order: dry spices (black and white pepper, tabia bun pepper, coriander, cloves, nutmeg), roots (galangal, turmeric, ginger), candlenuts, shallots and garlic, chillies, sea salt and, finally, shrimp paste.

Balinese cooking is all about balance – of cooling and heaty foods, of taste sensations (spicy, salty, pungent, aromatic, tart, rich) and of varied textures, with punctuations of crunch and crispness. This attention to balance is not only good gastronomic sense, it's also a reflection of the medicinal properties attributed to food. Occult associations with food frequently appear in Bali's elaborate ceremonial offerings, which comprise mainly bits of food ornamented with palm leaf festoons and flowers. It is thought that the gods like roast duck and cakes, and that demons prefer pork, chillies and strong drink.

The chef

Worlds away from the realm of chilli-eating demons, Chris Salans was born in Washington, DC in 1970, the son of an American father and French mother. The family moved to Paris when he was two, and Chris grew up eating wonderful food. "Our family had a farm where we picked wild mushrooms, a house in the mountains where we hunted for wild blueberries and a house by the sea where we caught fresh crabs and other things," he recalls. "My parents also loved to eat out. Every holiday we would get on a train or plane and travel to Vienna or Rome, or some great city in Europe, where the highlight was to go out to dinner. From the time I was eight years old, my parents took me with them. I grew up immersed in a rich food culture."

Chris started a degree in biology at Tufts University in Boston – his father hoped he would become a doctor – but after his first year, Chris realised his calling was to become a chef. "My father said, 'I'll cut a deal with you. Finish college and then you can go to culinary school.'" True to his word, after graduation, Chris enrolled in Le Cordon Bleu in Paris while preparing for his medical school examinations. "One thing led to another," says Chris, and the upshot was he took an internship – not in a hospital but at the (then) three-Michelin-starred restaurant, L'Oustau de Baumanière, in Les Baux de Provence, France. Chris later joined the three-Michelin-starred Lucas Carton in Paris, where he rose from the ranks to become head saucier. "The pressure of working in a kitchen was horrible. I loved it."

In the early 1990s, Chris returned to the US to learn more about the gastronomic scene and found himself working as a sous chef for David Bouley in New York. In 1995, Chris accompanied Bouley to Thailand for a cooking exhibition and he became so besotted with Asian cuisine that shortly afterwards, he accepted an offer to become executive chef at the luxury all-suite hotel The Legian in Bali, Indonesia, without actually knowing where Bali was. "It took me a while sitting with a map to find it; this little dot way over in Southeast Asia."

To this day, long-time residents of Bali still remember the excitement in the air when Chef Salans was helming the restaurant at The Legian. Word got around very quickly that, at last, one could find serious fine dining in Bali, and expatriates swarmed to the restaurant to see what the fuss was about.

While Chris was at The Legian, he met his future wife, Erni, who is from Semarang in

Central Java. That meant big phone bills when Chris returned to New York in 1997 to work with Bouley as head chef at the new Bouley's Bakery. Before long, he was granted six days' leave to dash back to Indonesia and marry Erni. He recalls: "We spent days in Jakarta filling in visa forms, then rushed to Semarang for a two-day wedding, then I was back in New York working a hundred hours a week." Erni joined him in New York soon afterwards. A year later, the couple moved to Napa Valley, California, where Chris worked with Thomas Keller (of The French Laundry) as head chef at Keller's new French bistro, Bouchon.

"But I was bitten by the Bali bug and married to an Indonesian; I had Bali in my heart." After trying to set up his own restaurant in the US and having little success finding an investor, Chris went to Bali to look for inspiration. In 1998, he helped launch the new incarnation of a restaurant in Ubud called Ary's Warung with Odeck Ariawan, a young local entrepreneur. Under Chris, Ary's Warung was transformed into a new creature with a cuisine that was unabashedly upscale and modern. About his cuisine at Ary's, Chris says, "I would ask my staff, who were all local, to cook a local dish for me and then I would reinterpret it in a modern way. It was experimental fusion but it taught me a lot about Indonesian cuisine."

Meanwhile, Chris's understanding of Indonesia was deepening. In the intervening years, Chris and Erni's two children were born: Nicolas Saputra, in Jakarta, in April 2000, and Laura Putri, in Semarang, in August 2002. Erni's mother came to stay with them while the children were still babies. "My mother-in-law is a marvellous cook," says Chris. "She helped me discover the world of Central Javanese cuisine. The amazing new flavours and ingredients opened my eyes and showed me there was more to Indonesian cuisine than what my staff knew. I was discovering Indonesian home cooking – a completely different and amazing, but unfortunately unknown, cuisine that I was learning to incorporate into my own."

But Chris's creative adventure was only just taking off. "The truth was that I was tired of bistro cuisine and wanted to push to a new level and do gastronomy instead of fusion. That's when I decided to open my own place." In July 2001, Chris set about establishing Mozaic.

Mozaic: the early days

Mozaic was created by Chris almost single-handedly. With little money in his pocket, he set forth with modest plans: find an existing building, buy a few tables and chairs, and start cooking. After several days of looking around, he found a beautiful location that was a former meditation temple. "Later, I found out it had also been the trysting place for the previous owner and his mistress. It's kind of an *Eat, Pray, Love* story," he jokes.

The property occupied a third of an acre of land just north of Ubud village, and comprised several small buildings. There was a small reception area, a Balinese-style pavilion with a large verandah that would serve as the main dining room and an outbuilding that became the kitchen. Chris drove around Bali buying furnishings here and kitchen equipment there; he supervised renovations and landscaping, and recruited and trained staff. "I opened the restaurant very quickly because I didn't want to miss the high season. There were only six or seven weeks between the time I found the property and when I opened the restaurant on 15 August 2001," he says.

"When we opened, we were serving 10 covers a night. We had seven tables on the verandah and three in the garden. My staff consisted of five cooks and eight waiters. After a few months, we were serving 15 covers. Six months later, it was 20, and the number steadily went up. This slow increase in numbers was ideal because it allowed me to do everything I wanted to do, to take care of and develop the knowledge of my staff, and develop my own style of cuisine and propel Mozaic forward. You couldn't do that anywhere else. I've been so lucky to be able to grow gradually. Anywhere else in the world, you have to be where you want to get to on the night you open." Today, the restaurant serves 60 covers a night and has 80 staff.

Word of Mozaic travelled quickly among food aficionados in Bali and beyond the island, and soon people too famous to be named began to flock there. One of them was a former president of the Republic of Indonesia, who came with a team of food-tasters. "You know, like a king does? They had an assortment of testing equipment," recalls Chris. "I brought them into the kitchen and they saw what we were doing, and saw us tasting things. I chatted with them and fed them; in the end they didn't test anything," he recalls.

Three months after they opened, Mozaic was breaking even and it continued to grow despite a series of setbacks to tourism in Bali. "A month after we opened, the catastrophic 9/11 terrorist attack happened, then there were the Kuta bombings, followed by the SARS epidemic. But little by little, we improved the place. We bought a generator, brought in more staff, added tables and expanded the main buildings. I wanted to continually improve the experience we were offering our guests," Chris explains.

But the process was not a haphazard one. "I had a business plan and it called for a destination restaurant in Ubud. At the time, Ubud had a more sophisticated level of tourism than Kuta's." Indeed, since the 1930s, Ubud's visitors have been almost stereotypically known as seekers of authenticity, ready to pay well for seclusion, tranquillity and access to Bali's cultural life. "I wanted that special Balinese warmth you find in Ubud, but with a totally professional staff. I wanted the waitstaff to be able to not only recite the menu but to explain it, to understand the dishes and know how they're made and what's in them, to pronounce the wine names correctly. Everyone told me I was crazy to open a gastronomic restaurant in Ubud. They said it would never work. But I didn't care. Ubud was where my heart was and I was going to stay."

Chris introduced a rigorous training programme for his staff that ran for three hours per week, with tests that he designed and graded himself. "If someone didn't do well on the tests, they were demoted and their pay was docked. Those who did well, advanced." Weekly training continues until today, and every evening at five o'clock, an hour before opening, there is a meeting with the waitstaff to discuss menu changes, the wine pairings of the day and special requirements for particular guests.

Some staff advanced brilliantly. "I'm lucky that my restaurant manager, Cok Senajaya, showed an aptitude for wine. I had him taste different wines, got him books to read and took him to wine festivals in Melbourne and Singapore. He's become a fine sommelier and since 2006 we've been recognised by *Wine Spectator* with the Award for Excellence."

In the early years, Chris did everything himself: training, accounting, marketing, sourcing ingredients, designing the website, running the front of the house and, of course, cooking and running the kitchen. "Because I was so busy during the day, I couldn't get into the kitchen until 6pm, so my kitchen staff had to be ready." They would prepare a gamut of oils, syrups, sauces and vegetables – some 42 to 48 pans – which would allow Chris to come in and cook *à la minute*. "Those who could work at that crazy pace grew with us; they could understand and support the cuisine." A Balinese trainee, Wayan Sudiarsana, rose through focused hard work and is now the sous chef.

The cuisine of Mozaic

The cuisine itself was also evolving. Chris says that for Mozaic, the years 2001 to 2003 were the most experimental. "I learned from David Bouley that a certain amount of chaos and spontaneity breeds creativity." When Mozaic opened, there was an à la carte menu and a tasting menu, with Chris experimenting with whatever new and intriguing ingredients happened to come in that day. "Sometimes it worked, sometimes it didn't. Sometimes it was fabulous, and sometimes it was more confusion than fusion." But it was the innovative use of Indonesian ingredients that was beginning to give Mozaic's cuisine its particular distinction. "My technique is modern French. I cook what I know, what I like and what I have. The big adventure at Mozaic has been the process of discovering new ingredients and flavours, and incorporating them into French techniques."

In 2007, Mozaic's culinary evolution was developed further by a new hire: young English chef James Ephraim, who is now chef de cuisine. James had cooked for the Duke of Westminster and had trained at the venerable Grosvenor Hotel in London, where he became a sous chef at the age of 20. He took the next year off to travel and

THIS PAGE FROM LEFT **Chris and sommelier Cok Senajaya working on food and wine pairings; Chris and the team celebrating Mozaic's anniversary; Chris showing students how to plate desserts during a professional cooking class.** OPPOSITE **Chris at home with his wife Erni and two children Nicolas and Laura.**

Carved Balinese doors and windows catch the light at the entrance to Mozaic, with a view through the foyer to the garden.

in Australia, James worked at the Lizard Island Resort on the Great Barrier Reef. In New Zealand, he opened the acclaimed Bracu Restaurant at Auckland's Simunovich Olive Estate. Chris says, "James brings an understanding and respect for my cuisine, and he's developed it and made it more beautiful and elegant." Recently, James travelled in Europe to research the latest cooking techniques and has introduced the technique of crystallisation to Mozaic. One of the new dishes James and Chris are most pleased with is the celeriac ice cream with black truffle honey topped with crystallised celeriac.

Daring infuses every aspect of Mozaic's cuisine. "We had a gorgonzola ice cream once," Chris recalls. "You serve it with figs in a red wine reduction and it makes a nice cheese course, but we ended up taking it even further and adding a chocolate fondant with strawberries braised with rosemary. It was insanely good but it wasn't for everyone. I served this dessert every night for a year, but now and again a guest would have it and say that the dish didn't make any sense. It's impossible to please everyone, so I have decided to please myself; what tastes good to me is what's on the menu."

Chris encourages people to adopt his techniques and apply them creatively. "Like the *rendang* oil we use in our beef carpaccio." Here, the spices for this classic Sumatran beef curry are roasted, ground and simmered for several hours in oil that becomes a marinade for the raw beef. "You can do this with any spice mixture from any country – Mexico, anywhere. Roast the spices, cook them slowly in oil and use the oil to flavour a dish. You use it with its traditional companion – in this case, *rendang* spices and beef – but you modernise it by, say, serving it raw."

Quality and service par excellence

Sourcing local ingredients had been a passion of Chris from the time he first arrived in Bali to work at The Legian. "You go to the market and you see the usual vegetables – cabbage, carrots and all that, but I wanted the rare things that people get from the forest and their backyards. Other chefs weren't taking advantage of all the wonderful stuff here. I went to the fish markets and found that most of the best fish was being exported. No one used butterfish then. We used it at The Legian and now it's everywhere." Chris got his personal driver to go out and look for special ingredients. Pak Ketut is still with him today at Mozaic, tasked exclusively with sourcing ingredients.

This entails more than seeking out the exotic. Chris insists on stringent quality control for all ingredients. "Take eggs, for instance," says Chris. "Eggs shouldn't be exposed to sunlight as it changes their flavour, but in Bali, they're driven around all day in an open truck. So every week, our driver goes to a farm three hours drive away to pick up a supply of eggs at six in the morning and puts them directly into refrigeration."

One might expect a gastronomic chef like Chris to be a quality control freak. In his case, it extends to all aspects of the business, and especially to guaranteeing the quality of the dining experience for guests, not only with regards to the food, but from when they make their reservation until they leave the restaurant. "We do everything we can to anticipate what people need to be entirely comfortable, and to guide them through a very special evening."

Eventually, Chris did away with the à la carte menu and instituted tasting menus. This came about in 2004 when Mozaic was invited to become a member of Les Grandes Tables du Monde (The Grand Tables of the World),

FROM TOP LEFT CLOCKWISE A secret mix of Balinese spices used to make the famous *babi guling* – spit-roasted whole suckling pig; Fresh cloves and clove flowers in bloom are a common sight in Bali; Market vendor selling just some of the many ingredients used in Balinese spice mixtures; Ripe jackfruit on the tree; Mounds of sea salt, produced in Bali's several salt-making centres, where sea water is evaporated in split coconut logs on the beach; Harvested soyabeans, the primary ingredient in tofu and tempeh; A beachside fish vendor selling his family's catch; A nutmeg fruit on the tree – the source of nutmeg and mace, spices that were highly sought after by early European explorers.

Chris and his team training in the Workshop.

Traditions & Qualité – so far only the second restaurant in Southeast Asia to achieve this distinction. The association was founded in 1954 by a group of French restaurateurs and presently lists 144 restaurants in 23 countries. Its logo comes from the drawing of a rooster by Jean Cocteau on a tablecloth at the Grand Véfour.

Chris says, "That was a big turning point for Mozaic and a big change for me. I hesitated for a month. Did I want to take the restaurant to this level? It was a very big step. I changed the tablecloths, the dinnerware, the glasses; I put in a small lounge. It meant a lot to me. It wasn't just, oh, I'm in this French guidebook, cool."

Chris was anxious that Mozaic fulfil the expectations of Les Grandes Tables du Monde, Traditions & Qualité. "We made sure every dish was gastronomic, that every dish had an element of surprise. You couldn't just have steak and salad on the menu." Offering only tasting menus was the solution to ensuring every customer had a Traditions & Qualité experience. The tasting menus have also evolved and there are presently four six-course menus that exemplify Mozaic's cuisine. There is a Discovery Menu, with an emphasis on using Indonesian ingredients, with modern Western presentation. Before the meal, diners are presented with a platter of the key Indonesian ingredients used in the dishes, allowing guests to examine, sniff and even nibble them. The Chef's Tasting Menu features classic Mozaic dishes, depending on availability of ingredients, both local and imported. There is a Vegetarian Menu, which also includes specialities such as homemade pasta, gnocchi and baked tortes. Finally, the Surprise Menu, which is based on the individual customer's preferences and incorporates the finest imported ingredients – such as caviar, foie gras, truffles and other speciality ingredients – and interprets them in Mozaic's own style.

Being listed with Les Grandes Tables du Monde, Traditions & Qualité did wonders for Mozaic's reputation, both internationally and in Bali. "A lot of people in Bali didn't quite understand us before that," says Chris. It also meant building a wine list – an impressive list of some 180 wines – a tremendous investment in Indonesia, which imposes high customs duties on imported wines and spirits. One constant that remained unchanged was the number of covers. "When Mozaic began to be consistently booked out in 2004, people said I should expand. I decided not to add any more tables but instead I increased my prices so that I could offer better ingredients and services to my guests. I wanted to be able to buy lobsters instead of prawns."

This decision meant Chris could focus on quality and value, and it paid off with Mozaic ranked by San Pellegrino as the 84th-best restaurant in the world in 2009. Mozaic has also been voted one of Asia's top six restaurants by *The Miele Guide* for three years running since 2008.

New directions

A significant change came the following year when one of the owners of Miele, a maker of high-end professional kitchen equipment, approached Mozaic with a view to a collaboration. "They asked me what I'd like to do. I said I'd like to teach." So the partnership began: Chris would build the space for a culinary school and Miele would provide the equipment. "The concept was for two dynamic companies to work together and create a unique synergy," says Chris. The result was the Workshop, a new air-conditioned building behind the restaurant with a stylish, professional kitchen and a comfortable space with sofas and dining tables. It also functions as a venue for private events and Chef's Table evenings, where people can watch the chef prepare their dinner in an informal atmosphere. "It's about 30 percent classroom and 70 percent dining." The Workshop also has a catering component.

"My goal with the Workshop was to create a centre in Southeast Asia for professionals to share knowledge about supplies, techniques and general tradecraft," says Chris. "We already have chefs coming from the big cities in Java – Bandung, Jakarta and Surabaya – as well as some from Singapore. It keeps growing."

Since then, other partners have joined Mozaic, including Vinoti Living, a retailer of furniture and home accessories, Schott Zwiesel, a glassware producer, and other purveyors of professional kitchen and dining equipment. These form part of an expanding professional network and have led

Wine Spectator AWARD OF EXCELLENCE

LES GRANDES TABLES DU MONDE TRADITIONS & QUALITÉ

Mozaic has won *Wine Spectator*'s Award of Excellence every year since 2006, and is a member of Les Grandes Tables du Monde – Traditions & Qualité.

FROM LEFT Chef de cuisine James Ephraim at work; Chris and his former pastry chef, François Seurin, who had an huge influence on Mozaic's cuisine.

to invitations for Chris to do cooking presentations in Germany, Japan, Australia, Spain and Thailand.

The Workshop fulfils Chris's passion for sharing what he knows. Outside the Workshop is a small botanical garden with local spices and fruit trees. Some of the classes begin in the garden so students can see where ingredients come from and how they grow. The cooking classes are immaculately planned and organised, with deft support staff on hand to help students, and they conclude with a superb meal and a bag of gifts.

Remarkably, Chris is happy to share his knowledge with other chefs in Bali. "It's partly to teach others about what we've achieved here at Mozaic, and partly to teach how to use the imported ingredients suppliers bring in. I do it for fun and inspiration." He also helps plan menus for other restaurants, displaying the same creative zeal he brings to everything he does.

In 2008, Mozaic opened its lounge. "We wanted to offer guests more than just a dining experience. We wanted them to enjoy themselves before or after dinner in a special area where they can relax with a cigar or cigarette (the restaurant is non-smoking) and a cocktail in hand. I put a lot of thought into the bar and developed a creative array of beverages based around local seasonal ingredients. To accompany these, James Ephraim and I created a menu of tapas-like dishes based on Mozaic's cuisine. We now have a live jazz band playing several nights a week. Some guests just come for the tapas and drinks."

The people behind the scenes

Although Chris is clearly the main driver of Mozaic, he is quick to acknowledge the wonderful people around him, some of whom have been with him from the beginning. "One of the greatest influences on my cooking was French pastry chef François Seurin, who was with us from 2005 to 2007. There was a huge creative synergy between us with a large amount of exchange between our realms – between savoury and sweet. About 80 percent of our desserts are François' creations." One of th emore remarkable example of this exchange was a Guinness beer sauce. "We wanted to soften the harshness of the beer, so we decided to add some fruit. We cooked prunes in a beer sauce and then created a dessert with roast peaches, coriander- and vanilla-braised endives, and a lemon verbena sorbet. We essentially took two traditional combinations – beer with endives, and lemon verbena with peaches – and put them together."

As Mozaic has grown, so has its administration. Its general manager is Nicola Scaramuzzino, a geology graduate from the University of Pisa, who gained extensive sales, marketing and management experience while working with hotels and travel agencies in Bali. "Nicola has brought a new energy to Mozaic," says Chris. "With Nicola by my side, the help of my invaluable accountant, Pak Putu, and the kitchen doing brilliantly under Chef Ephraim, I can now think about expanding Mozaic. Not expanding outwards, but from within and doing more exciting things with the Mozaic brand: our cookbook, a TV show, welcoming guest chefs, participating in international gastronomic events, doing catering – the possibilities are infinite."

RATIONAL
mozaic

A DAY IN THE LIFE OF MOZAIC

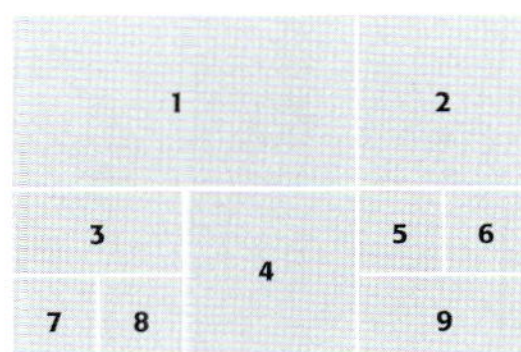

1. Mozaic's garden where local fruit, spices and aromatic herbs are grown for guests to sample during cooking classes and private dinners in the Workshop.
2. *Left to right*: general manager Nicola Scaramuzzino, Chris Salans and James Ephraim discuss the evening's guest list.
3. Daily arrivals of fresh fruit and vegetables influence Chris and James in their creation of new culinary delights.
4. Chef de cuisine James Ephraim conducting a cooking class in the Workshop.
5. Breads and rolls are baked fresh every morning.
6. Kitchen staff preparing for the evening.
7. Planning menus and wine pairings. Each dish on the menu is carefully paired with a wine so guests may enjoy thoughtfully selected wines with each of the menus served at Mozaic.
8. Imported kitchenware is at the heart of the French technique underlying Mozaic's cuisine.
9. Tables are set in the afternoon with great care.

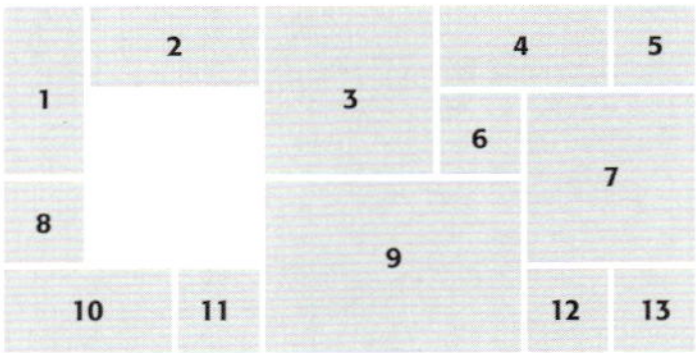

1. Upon arrival, guests are shown into the Mozaic lounge for a drink and complimentary canapés while looking over the night's menu.
2. In the kitchen, fresh herbs and flowers are set out ready to be used as garnishes.
3. The dining table at a Mozaic private dinner, held in the Workshop, where Chris or James cook for the guests.
4. A table in the pavilion where guests dine on the covered verandah overlooking the beautiful Mozaic gardens.
5. Weddings, birthdays and anniversaries are thoughtfully accompanied by beautiful and tasteful cakes prepared by Mozaic's pastry team.
6. Petits fours and coffee or tea signal the end of a wonderful meal.
7. Chris in action in his Miele kitchen, cooking for a private group of diners in the Mozaic Workshop.
8. The garden, where guests dine outdoors amongst the lush greenery and under the wonderful night sky of Bali.
9. The Mozaic lounge where guests are invited to pre- and post-dinner drinks while listening to some jazz. The lounge also offers a tapas-style menu for those who would prefer a casual nibble.
10. The bar where cocktails and mixed drinks are created, using the same innovative approach Chris applies to his cuisine.
11. Chris and James work together daily to create new recipes.
12. Pots and bains maries filled with sauces – the true secret of French cuisine.
13. A table on the verandah of Mozaic's dining pavilion.

Miele

RAWON
QUAIL

Verdant terraces as far as the eye can see near Ubud. In the foreground is a shrine to Dewi Sri, the Balinese Rice Goddess.

VANILLA BEAN

Vanilla planifolia (or *V. fragrans*) (*Orchidaceae*)
Indonesian/Balinese: *panili*

CHARACTER

Vanilla has an unforgettable flavour – rich, fragrant, sweet, slightly smoky and voluptuous. The Indonesian vanilla bean is slightly smaller and thinner than other varieties, such as Mexican, Madagascan, West Indian and Tahitian. It has a characteristic aroma, less intense than those of other vanillas, but it's sweet and floral, with a lingering taste that gives it a versatility other more powerful vanillas don't have. It costs 25 percent less than other vanillas.

PHYSICALS

The vanilla bean is the fruit of an orchid native to Mexico, where it was first cultivated by the Mesoamerican Totonaca people. Although there are over a hundred vanilla orchids, only the cultivar *Vanilla planifolia* produces the vanilla bean used in cooking. The bean pod is filled with a thick paste of tiny seeds in a dark red liquid from which the extract is produced. Vanilla grows best in equatorial climates at an elevation from sea level up to 1,500 metres. The world's largest producer is Madagascar, followed by Indonesia, where it's grown on the islands of Flores, Java and Sulawesi.

LOCAL USE

Vanilla was introduced to Indonesia as a cash crop in the 19th century, and appears in certain Indonesian recipes that have a European influence or ancestry, such as those for custards, cakes and other sweets.

NOTES FROM CHEF SALANS

Vanilla is a versatile ingredient as it can be matched with both savoury and sweet dishes: fish, shellfish and meats as well as desserts. In the recipes found in this book, vanilla is paired with seafood, in both a cold and hot preparation. Vanilla is generally considered an expensive ingredient but because it grows so abundantly in Indonesia, it's readily available and very affordable. Besides the vanilla bean, another great product from the vanilla plant is the flower, which has a distinct characteristic flavour without being sweet. This makes it an interesting ingredient to use, either on its own in raw dishes, or as an infusion in a hot dish.

Selecting the ingredient: Look for vanilla beans that are moist, dark and plump. Vanilla that is dry and hard may have been overdried or stored for too long. Most vanilla beans that have a nice aroma will do the job. All have different characteristics – some cost 10 times more than others – but a moist, plump and nice-smelling vanilla will always deliver a good result.

How to prepare it: Slice the pod lengthwise and scrape out the tiny black seeds. The vanilla pod can be used along with the seeds for additional flavour (though it needs to be discarded before serving). Alternatively, infusing a jar of salt or sugar with the vanilla pod will result in delicately perfumed salt and sugar that you can use in most recipes.

Substitutes: Fresh vanilla bean can be substituted with vanilla extract, although the flavour is not exactly the same. One vanilla bean should be replaced with approximately 1 tsp of pure vanilla extract. Don't confuse artificial vanilla essence with the pure extract: the former is made from synthetic vanillin, is much cheaper and lacks complexity.

OPPOSITE Fragrant dried vanilla beans, the fruit of the *Vanilla planifolia* orchid, are gathered for sorting after harvest.
THIS PAGE Good vanilla beans are plump, dark and moist.

mozaic of cuttlefish and exotic fruits vanilla dressing

ABOUT THE RECIPE: This was one of the very first Mozaic dishes and one of my favourites. It's a literal mosaic of different ingredients, and its unusual combination of fruits and cuttlefish gives the dish a refreshing flavour. The dressing is a delightful concoction of fresh, local ingredients, including green peppercorns, vanilla beans and star anise. The key to this dish is having both sweet (eg fruit) and acidic (eg lemon juice) elements to balance out the flavours.

*Elements of this recipe should be prepared at least 1 week in advance.

PORTION: Serves 6 as an appetiser **DIFFICULTY LEVEL:**

INGREDIENTS

Vanilla Dressing *
1 tbsp fresh green peppercorns
½ tsp star anise, seeds only
75 ml salad oil
1 vanilla bean, seeds only

Cuttlefish
1 cuttlefish (whole weight approx 650 g, cleaned weight approx 300 g)
2 tbsp olive oil
salt and white pepper, to taste

Fruit
50 g papaya
50 g watermelon
50 g mango

Caramelised Walnuts
7 walnuts, roasted
5 tsp sugar

Condiments and Garnishes
6 green asparagus
½ tsp chives, sliced
salt and white pepper, to taste
lemon juice, to taste
6 fresh herb sprigs of your choice

* This makes 4 times the quantity needed in this recipe. The remaining dressing can be stored in the refrigerator for several months.

METHOD

Make the vanilla dressing in advance. Place all the ingredients in a blender and process until smooth. Store in an airtight container and keep in a dark, cool place for a minimum of 1 week.

To cook the cuttlefish, heat a grill or grill pan until it's very hot. Place the olive oil, salt and pepper on a plate or tray and roll the cuttlefish in the mixture, ensuring it's well coated. Place it on the hot grill then put a heavy object, such as a heavy pan, on it to ensure the cuttlefish doesn't curl up while cooking. Once you have nice grill marks on one side (2–3 minutes), turn the cuttlefish over and repeat the process on the other side. Refrigerate. Once cold, cut the cuttlefish into 1½ x 1½ cm squares. Cut the fruit to the same size and thickness as the cuttlefish. You will need 8 squares of cuttlefish and 8 squares of mixed fruits for each portion.

To prepare the walnuts, stir the sugar over medium heat until it melts and caramelises to a dark brown colour (approximately 5 minutes). Remove it from the heat and add the walnuts, quickly tossing them in the pan to ensure they are well coated in the caramel. Remove the walnuts from the pan one by one so they don't stick together, and place them on a sheet of waxed paper. When cold, cut or break the walnuts into small pieces.

To prepare the asparagus, remove any brown ends, then peel and cut each asparagus into 3 pieces (1 tip and 2 pieces of stem). Blanch the asparagus in boiling salted water, then plunge them into a bowl of ice-cold water to stop the cooking process and retain their lovely green colour. Drain and set aside.

To assemble, mix the squares of cuttlefish and fruit with 2 tbsp of vanilla dressing in a bowl and season with salt, pepper and lemon juice to taste. Arrange the squares on the plates in a chequerboard pattern (see photo opposite).

Put the asparagus in the same bowl that previously held the cuttlefish and fruit, and mix well with the dressing left over in the bowl. Place a tsp of the walnut pieces on each plate, then arrange the asparagus on top. Mix the chives with another tbsp of dressing and drizzle it around the plate for decoration. Garnish with a fresh herb sprig and serve immediately.

TIPS

At Mozaic, we cook our cuttlefish sous vide (in a vacuum bag), but it's also possible to cook it on a grill, as in this recipe. To stop the cuttlefish from curling when grilling, simply place a heavy object, such as a pan, on it to ensure it stays flat. Once done, the cuttlefish may seem a little undercooked, but if you rest it at room temperature for several minutes, it will cook through and become moist and tender.

For information on making a caramel, see Techniques (page 140).

vanilla-roasted gindara, braised endives and wild mushrooms with grape-red wine reduction and aromatic ginger sauce

ABOUT THE RECIPE: This dish is a tribute to David Bouley, for whom I worked for a long time. He's the chef who influenced me the most and turned me into the cook I am today. He had (and probably still has) a terrible habit of making last-minute decisions and changes to the menu. This always created panic in the kitchen and sometimes left guests waiting for their dishes. Back then, I never understood why he did that but today, as a chef, I understand. No matter how much it makes others unhappy, spontaneity results in creativity, and induces continuously bright and surprising flavours in the kitchen. Only someone with a trained palate can have clear perception amidst the chaos of a busy restaurant kitchen, but I have stuck to David's principle (or should I say "ill-logic") ever since and it has served me well.

PORTION: Serves 6 as an appetiser or 3 as a main course **DIFFICULTY LEVEL:**

INGREDIENTS

Red Wine Reduction
1 lobster head or 10 prawn heads
3 cloves garlic, roasted, see Techniques (page 140)
375 ml good pinot noir
500 g dark muscat-style grapes
salt, to taste

Endives
1 tsp coriander seeds
35 g butter
300 g Belgian endives, leaves picked, core discarded
1 vanilla bean, seeds only
1 tsp icing sugar
salt and white pepper, to taste

Ginger Sauce
1 tbsp soya sauce
1 tbsp balsamic vinegar
1 tsp tomato ketchup
100 g cold butter, cubed
salt, to taste
100 g ginger, juiced

Mushrooms
2 tbsp salad oil
25 g butter
300 g seasonal wild mushrooms, cleaned
salt and white pepper, to taste
2 pinches thyme leaves
2 tbsp shallots, chopped

Fish
480 g gindara fillet, 6 x 80 g or 3 x 160 g portions
1½ vanilla beans, split
salt and white pepper, to taste
2 tbsp salad oil
50 g butter
sea salt, to taste

Garnish
6 fresh herb sprigs of your choice

METHOD

To make the red wine reduction, roast the garlic and lobster head in a 180°C oven until lightly browned. Place them in a large saucepan with the grapes, wine and a pinch of salt. Bring to the boil and simmer gently until all the grapes have popped open. Strain through a coarse sieve and push down on the mixture to extract all the juices. Reduce the sauce so it's slightly thick and suitable for drizzling on a plate. Strain through a fine-meshed strainer, then season to taste with salt and a little red wine as needed.

To prepare the endives, dry roast the coriander seeds in a pan until they're fragrant, then lightly crush them. In a large pan, melt the butter over medium heat. When it's hot and bubbling, add the endives, icing sugar, coriander seeds and vanilla seeds. Allow the endives to cook gently until they are golden-brown and caramelised evenly. Season with salt and pepper, then set aside.

For the ginger sauce, put the soya sauce, balsamic vinegar and tomato ketchup in a saucepan and stir to combine. Bring to the boil, then take off the heat. Add the cold butter 1 tbsp at a time, whisking continuously. As you add the butter, the sauce will cool. Keep the sauce warm by placing the pan over a hot water bath or close to (but not over) the stove-top flame, and continue to add the butter. When all the butter has been incorporated, season to taste with salt and then add the ginger juice. Keep the sauce warm in the hot water bath until you are ready to serve. The ginger flavour will be slightly overpowering, but don't worry – only a very small amount of this sauce is used.

To prepare the mushrooms, heat the oil and butter in a pan over medium heat. When the butter begins to bubble, add the mushrooms and allow them to colour lightly all over, then add salt and pepper to taste. Add the shallots and thyme, and remove from the heat so the shallots don't burn. Allow the shallots to cook gently in the residual heat of the pan. Keep warm.

To cook the fish, preheat the oven to 180°C. Split the vanilla beans in half, and cut the whole bean in half lengthwise; you should have 6 pieces. Season the fish portions with salt and pepper, and poke a piece of vanilla into each portion so that it goes through the fish. Heat the oil in an ovenproof pan and when it begins to lightly smoke, add the fish. Place the pan in the hot oven and bake for 6 minutes. Remove from the oven and add the butter to the pan, basting the fish with the hot butter. Remove the fish from the pan, season with sea salt and prepare to serve immediately.

To assemble, place a spoonful of the red wine reduction in the centre of each preheated plate or bowl. Place a spoonful of the endives on the reduction and a piece of fish on top. Top the fish with the mushrooms. Using a hand blender, emulsify the ginger sauce to lighten it and create a light foam. Place a spoonful of foam on top of each fish portion. Garnish with a fresh herb sprig and serve immediately.

TIP

Gindara has different names all over the world. In Australia it's called butterfish, in the US it's called escolar; here in Bali it's called *ikan setan*, which oddly means "satan fish" (I'm not really sure why), and in Japan it's called *shiro*. It's an extremely rich and fatty fish that is very difficult to overcook. It's a great fish to roast or grill as it remains moist longer than most other types of fish.

CASSIA BARK

Cinnamomum cassia (L.) Presl (*Lauraceae*)
(Variety: Indonesian cassia [*Cinnamomum burmanni*])
Indonesian/Balinese: *kulit kasia*
Malay: *kaya manis*
Also known as: *bastard cinnamon*, *Canton cassia*, or *Chinese cinnamon*

CHARACTER

Cassia bark has a warm, sweetish taste and an aroma that is similar to cinnamon, but is stronger, with earthy and slightly bitter notes. This makes it especially suitable for savoury dishes and adds character when used in a sweet context.

PHYSICALS

The tree that cassia bark comes from grows to a height of approximately 15 metres. It has hard, elongated leaves that are reddish when young. In appearance, dried cassia is similar to cinnamon, but with a heavier, coarser bark that is slightly greyish in colour and very hard. The inside of the bark is smoother and reddish-brown. Cinnamon sticks roll into a single quill, while cassia is rolled from both sides towards the centre, like a scroll. Based on fragrance only, most people can't tell the difference between the two. As cinnamon is less commonly grown, it's more expensive than cassia.

LOCAL USE

Cassia is used in savoury Indonesian dishes, such as *rendang* (a spicy dry beef or chicken curry), and in desserts such as *kolak*, which is made with palm sugar and coconut milk. Cassia bark has medicinal properties similar to cinnamon's; it's a tonic and stimulant and helps relieve gas; in its oil form, cassia and cinnamon have antibacterial properties.

NOTES FROM CHEF SALANS

The recipes here show the versatility of cassia bark. Not only is it suitable for both savoury and sweet dishes, it can also be used in different ways. You can infuse it whole, grind it or add it to vinegars; the number of interesting techniques and creative uses for this spice is endless.
Selecting the ingredient: Choose cassia bark sticks that exude an aroma without having to break or rub them. Be sure they have no mould; cassia bark develops mould fairly quickly.
How to prepare it: Cassia bark requires no preparation. You can use it as is and infuse it into your dishes. If you want a more subtle flavour, grind it into a powder but be careful how much you put in — I find the powder can add a certain bitterness. For that reason, I suggest using the whole bark.
Substitutes: Cinnamon can be used as a substitute. Avoid using pre-ground powders where possible; they can be overpowering.

OPPOSITE Cassia bark is harvested from the *Cinnamomum cassia* tree, native to Indonesia.
THIS PAGE Unlike cinnamon, which forms a single quill, cassia bark usually forms a double scroll-like curl.

chocolate mousse with cassia bark, cocoa crisps and kumquats

ABOUT THE RECIPE: This dish was created after I spent a weekend in the Banda Islands, which are part of Maluku, or the Moluccas, the fabled "Spice Islands" of yesteryear. Cassia trees grow in abundance there, and the aroma as you walk through a forest of these trees is just incredible. My idea was to create a chocolate mousse that, when served at room temperature, would be reminiscent of a chocolate *moelleux* (molten chocolate) with a liquid centre. We have tried to play with textures in an interesting way, so the centre of the dessert is a very light, runny jelly, and the mousse on the outside is as light as air. The technique used to create the chocolate mousse is unusual, and although the dish is time-consuming to make, it's well worth the effort, as this dessert is truly divine.

*Elements of this recipe should be prepared 1 day in advance.

PORTION: Serves 10 **DIFFICULTY LEVEL:** 🍴🍴🍴

INGREDIENTS

Jelly
200 ml milk
25 cm cassia bark, broken into pieces
1 egg yolk
1 tsp white sugar
120 g milk chocolate, chopped
½ leaf gelatine, pre-soaked

Kumquat Candy
20 kumquats
200 g liquid glucose
70 g white sugar
250 ml water
10 threads Spanish saffron

Chocolate Lady Fingers
3 eggs, separated
50 g sugar
50 g plain flour, sifted
5½ tsp cocoa powder, sifted

Mousse
5 egg yolks
5 tsp white sugar
200 ml milk
60 g dark chocolate, chopped
140 g milk chocolate, chopped
1½ leaves gelatine, pre-soaked
200 ml cream

Chocolate Spray
150 g cocoa butter
150 g dark compound chocolate, chopped

Cocoa Crisps
70 g white rice, cooked
5 tsp white sugar
2 tbsp glutinous rice flour
1 tsp orange zest, finely grated
3 tsp cocoa powder

METHOD

Make the jelly in advance. Bring the milk and cassia bark to the boil, then take it off the heat, cover and allow to infuse for 20 minutes. Make a sabayon by beating the egg yolk and sugar together in a stainless-steel mixing bowl over a pan of simmering water until the mixture is thick and smooth (5–10 minutes). Reheat the cassia milk to 80°C and add it to the sabayon, mixing well. Gradually add the chocolate, stirring until it has completely melted. Add the gelatine and stir until it has dissolved. Strain the liquid and let it sit at room temperature until it just starts to set (this should occur at approximately 20°C), then pour into the smaller moulds and freeze.

Make the kumquat candy in advance. Prick each kumquat 6 to 10 times with a toothpick or skewer. Combine the glucose, sugar and water, and bring to the boil over low heat. Add the kumquats and cover with parchment paper, pressing it lightly onto the surface of the liquid. Simmer gently until the kumquats are cooked through and translucent in colour. This should take a minimum of 1½ hours. If needed, add more water so the syrup doesn't get too thick.

Once the kumquats are cooked, cool to room temperature and strain. Return the syrup to the heat, add the saffron threads and bring to the boil. Dilute with water, and adjust the consistency of the syrup so it's suitable for drizzling on a plate. Place the candied kumquats back in the saffron syrup and refrigerate. Allow the fruit to marinate for at least 12 hours.

To make the chocolate lady fingers, preheat the oven to 160°C. Beat the egg whites and sugar until stiff peaks form (like a meringue). Beat the egg yolks to break them, then add them to the meringue and fold them in gently. Fold in the cocoa and flour. Using a spatula, spread the mixture (to a thickness of ½ cm) on a baking tray lined with a non-stick mat or baking paper. Bake at 160°C for approximately 8 minutes. Cool and then cut 10 6-cm circles using a cutter or one of the large moulds.

Start to assemble the dessert by placing the large moulds on a tray and lining the inside walls of each mould with plastic mica that has been cut to size. Then, place a circle of lady finger at the bottom of each mould. Remove the frozen jellies from their moulds, returning the de-moulded ones to the freezer until you have finished this task. Working quickly so the jellies don't begin to melt, place one frozen jelly in the centre of each mould, using melted chocolate to glue the jelly to the lady finger. Freeze until set.

To prepare the mousse, make a sabayon by beating the egg yolks and sugar together in a stainless-steel mixing bowl over a pan of simmering water until the mixture is thick and smooth (5–10 minutes). Bring the milk to the boil, then remove from the heat. Allow to cool for a few minutes until it reaches a temperature of approximately 80°C, then add the milk to the sabayon, mixing well. Add the chocolate, stirring until it has completely melted. Add the gelatine and stir until it has dissolved. Allow to cool to room temperature.

Almonds
60 g sliced almonds
5 tsp white sugar
2½ tsp coconut palm sugar
¼ tsp cassia bark powder
2 tsp egg white

Whipped Cream
125 ml cream
¼ leaf gelatine, pre-soaked

Garnishes
10 sprigs mint
100 g chocolate, melted

Special Equipment
10 moulds 2 cm wide x 3 cm tall*
10 moulds 6 cm wide x 4½ cm tall
plastic mica (a sturdy plastic sheet that can be cut into strips for lining the moulds)
chocolate spray gun

* It's all right to use different-sized moulds, but one should always be half the size of the other, and be able to fit inside it. If commercial moulds are not available, they can be made using PVC pipe.

Meanwhile, whip the cream to soft peaks. When the chocolate mousse mixture has cooled sufficiently (the mixture shouldn't set), add the whipped cream and fold it in. Don't overmix or the lightness of the whipped cream will be lost, but make sure the whipped cream has been fully incorporated into the chocolate with no lumps of whipped cream remaining. Place the mixture in a jug and pour it into the moulds so it fills the space around the jelly and covers it by at least 1 cm. Freeze until set.

To make the chocolate spray, melt the cocoa butter and chocolate in a mixing bowl over a pan of simmering water, stirring until the mixture is smooth. The mixture can be kept at room temperature until it's needed. When you are ready to use it, reheat it gently over a double boiler, pour it into a chocolate spray gun and use immediately. The mixture should be lukewarm to get the best result.

Remove the frozen mousses from the moulds, then gently remove the plastic mica. Using the spray gun, spray each mousse (while still frozen) so that it has a light, even covering of chocolate. Refrigerate. Please note: once the mousses have been sprayed with the chocolate mixture, they should be stored in the refrigerator. Do not freeze them.

For the cocoa crisps, preheat the oven to 110°C. Blend all the ingredients until smooth and then strain. Place a 4 cm x 8 cm x 1 mm thick silicone or plastic mould on a baking tray lined with a non-stick mat or baking paper. Using a spatula, spread a thin layer of the mixture inside the mould to form the shape of the crisp. Make as many crisps as the tray can contain and bake for 15 minutes. Flip the crisps over and bake for 1 hour or until brown. Remove from the tray and cool to room temperature and store in an airtight container.

To make the caramelised almonds, preheat the oven to 160°C. Gently combine all the ingredients in a large mixing bowl. Spread over a baking tray lined with a non-stick mat or baking paper. Bake for 20 minutes or until golden-brown. Remove and allow to cool to room temperature. Break into small pieces and store in an airtight container.

To prepare the whipped cream, dissolve the gelatine in a little heated cream (the smallest amount required). Mix it into the rest of the cream, then beat until soft peaks form. Refrigerate. Please note: in Bali, we use gelatine to ensure that whipped cream doesn't melt in the heat; this shouldn't be necessary in cooler climates.

Assembly
Remove the sprayed mousses from the refrigerator and make sure the jelly in each mousse has defrosted by gently inserting a toothpick into it. If the jelly is still frozen, let the mousses sit at room temperature until they have defrosted, then serve immediately or the mousse may break apart.

When ready to serve, decorate each plate with the melted chocolate, kumquat syrup and kumquats. Place a mousse on each plate. Top the mousse with a scoop, or quenelle, of whipped cream, a cocoa crisp, some caramelised almonds and a mint sprig. Serve immediately.

TORCH GINGER FLOWER

Etlingera elatior (*Zingiberaceae*)
Indonesian: *bunga kecombrang* (*kencong, kincung, asam tikala*)
Balinese: *kecicang*
Malay: *bunga kantan*
Thai: *kaalaa*

FOOD CHARACTER
The bright, peppery, floral taste of the torch ginger flower is one of the most surprising flavours in Southeast Asian cooking. It's used in Java, Sumatra, Bali and Thailand, and is also a common flavouring ingredient used in the cooking of the hybrid Straits Chinese or Nyonya cuisine of Indonesia, Malaysia and Singapore.

PHYSICALS
The striking red ginger plant itself, tall with leafy stalks, is thought to be native to Java. The flowers form inside a showy inflorescence that grows directly from the rhizome and, when immature, resembles a waxy pink pine cone. It's the bulb-like buds that are used as an ingredient. Two types of *kecicang* are found in Bali: one is pale pink – its flavour is more intense – and the other is a brighter pink. It's called torch ginger, not because it's related to the ginger family, but because the leaves resemble those of the ginger plant. Until the plant flowers, it looks very similar to a ginger plant.

LOCAL USE
In Bali, the bud (*kecicang*) (or alternatively, the very young shoot called *bongkot*) is used to make a spice paste called *sambal matah* (literally "raw sambal"), along with raw shallots, chillies, salt, lime leaves and roasted shrimp paste (*terasi*).

NOTES FROM CHEF SALANS
In the recipes that follow, the torch ginger flower is prepared in both the traditional Balinese way, as well as presented in a modern way that is illustrative of Mozaic's style of cuisine.
Selecting the ingredient: Since torch ginger is a flower, it should be purchased as fresh as possible. The flower should be plump and there should be no bruising or dryness on the outer petals. As it isn't always available in Asian markets, one can sometimes find it at a florist since the inflorescence, sometimes called Stone Rose, is a popular ornamental.
How to prepare it: The flower should be cut off from the stalk. The stalk, which has a lot of flavour, can be infused in a liquid. Remove one or two layers of the outer petals, then slice the flower in half vertically to expose the inside of the flower. The flower is then sliced crosswise very finely, starting from the tip of the flower and moving towards the stem. The tip has a more intense flavour than the stem end.
Substitutes: There are no substitutes for torch ginger; however, in these recipes, it can be replaced with a double to triple quantity of lemongrass.

OPPOSITE The torch ginger flower is a spectacular inflorescence, popular with florists.
THIS PAGE The bud of the torch ginger flower peeled and sliced lengthwise, ready for use.

ginger flower sorbet with fresh strawberries and lime leaves

ABOUT THE RECIPE: This is one of my favourite recipes as it really represents Mozaic's cuisine: isolating an exotic flavour from a quintessentially local dish and turning it into something unexpected, yet surprising, for both visitors and locals. This dish came about during the first few years I lived in Bali, when I'd order grilled prawns or fish from vendors along the beach. These would always be served with a perfectly ambrosial *sambal kecicang* (Balinese ginger flower relish). The first time I tried it, the flavour was so magical I had to ask what was in it. And I had my answer: torch ginger. It changed my life forever.

PORTION: Serves 10 **DIFFICULTY LEVEL:**

INGREDIENTS

Marinated Strawberries
250 g strawberries, hulled and cut into segments
2 large kaffir lime leaves, finely sliced
4 tbsp lemon juice
4 tbsp sugar

Sorbet
350 ml water
125 g sugar
100 g liquid glucose
1 medium ginger flower, finely sliced
1 ½ leaves gelatine, pre-soaked
150 ml plain unsweetened yoghurt
2–3 tbsp lemon juice

Garnish
10 kaffir lime leaves, whole
10 torch ginger petals

Special Equipment
ice cream machine

METHOD

Place the strawberries in a bowl and season with the sugar, lemon juice and lime leaves. Cover with cling film and allow to marinate in the refrigerator for a minimum of 1 hour and up to 24 hours.

Bring the water, glucose and sugar to the boil in a saucepan. Add the ginger flower and simmer for 1 minute. Remove from the heat, cover and allow the mixture to infuse for 10 minutes. Strain. Add the gelatine, stir well and allow the mixture to cool to room temperature and thicken to a soft set. Whisk in the yoghurt and lemon juice (to taste, depending the level of acidity, but I suggest slightly more rather then less lemon juice for perfect results). Mix until smooth. Chill the mixture in the refrigerator, and then churn the sorbet in an ice cream machine until it hardens. Transfer the sorbet to a plastic container and freeze for a minimum of 1 hour.

To serve, divide the marinated strawberries and liquid between 10 pre-chilled bowls. Place 1 scoop, or quenelle, of sorbet on top, garnish with a kaffir lime leaf and torch ginger petal and serve immediately.

TIPS

For information on how to make sorbet if you don't have an ice cream machine, see Techniques (page 140).

If strawberries are unavailable, the recipe works beautifully with seasonal fruit like peaches or apricots.

sesame-crusted tuna with tomato, belimbing wuluh and rosewater apple salad, and ginger flower relish

ABOUT THE RECIPE: There are many Balinese ingredients with subtle nuances of flavour that, on their own, are probably not complex enough to be the main star of a recipe. So I came up with a dish that features several local ingredients, each with a different texture and taste. By experimenting with different levels of acidity, bitterness and sweetness, I created the perfect tomato salad with the right balance of flavours. I also decided to top this salad with a modern interpretation of a traditional Balinese dish called *sambal be tongkol*, which is a delightful combination of tuna and ginger flower.

PORTION: Serves 4 as an appetiser or 2 as a main course **DIFFICULTY LEVEL:**

INGREDIENTS

Salad
160 g cherry tomatoes, halved
1 belimbing wuluh, finely sliced
2 rosewater apples, cut into segments
50 ml olive oil
2 tbsp red wine vinegar
1 tsp fresh ginger juice
1 tbsp fresh herbs, finely sliced (such as lemon basil)
1 tbsp shallots, finely chopped
1 tbsp chives or spring onions, finely sliced
salt and pepper, to taste

Relish
¼ tsp shrimp paste, toasted
¼ tsp salt
3 tbsp shallots, finely sliced
1 tbsp coconut oil
3 tbsp Lombok chillies (or red chillies), finely sliced
1 lemo lime leaf, finely sliced (or any edible lime leaf)
1 tbsp ginger flower, finely sliced
1 tbsp tomatoes, skinned and seeded, finely sliced
½ lemo lime (or any fragrant lime)
salt, to taste

Fish
320 g tuna fillet, 4 x 80 g or 2 x 160 g portions
salt and pepper, to taste
60 g white sesame seeds, untoasted
2 tbsp salad oil
1 tbsp sesame oil
sea salt, for garnish

Garnish
4 fresh herb sprigs of your choice

METHOD

To make the salad, place the cherry tomatoes, belimbing wuluh and rosewater apples in a bowl. Drizzle the olive oil, red wine vinegar and ginger juice over them. Add the herbs, shallots, chives, salt and pepper. Toss the ingredients and adjust the seasoning. Set aside for a minimum of 30 minutes.

For the relish, crumble the shrimp paste and salt together in a bowl. Please note: these steps must be followed precisely in order to achieve the correct balance of flavours. Add the shallots and half the coconut oil and, using your fingers in a light rubbing motion, combine the ingredients for 1 minute. Add the chilli and combine in the same manner for 1 minute, adding the remaining coconut oil as needed to ensure the mixture is moist enough. Repeat this process with the lime leaf, followed by the ginger flower. Finally, add the tomatoes and squeeze in the juice of the half lime, throwing the entire lime half into the mixture as well. Do a final toss and adjust the seasoning. Set aside.

To cook the tuna, season the tuna portions with salt and pepper on both sides, then lightly press the sesame seeds onto one side. Heat the salad oil and half the sesame oil in a frypan until lightly smoking, then place the tuna fillets, sesame seed side down, in the pan. Sear the tuna (on one side only) until the sesame seeds are golden-brown and the tuna is cooked to your liking (at Mozaic, we serve our tuna rare). Remove from the pan and drain on paper towels.

To serve, heap the tomato salad in the centre of each plate. Place the fish on top, sesame-crusted side facing up. Sprinkle with sea salt and the remaining sesame oil. Top with the ginger flower relish (discarding the lime half) and a fresh herb sprig. Serve immediately.

TIP

Some of these ingredients may not be available where you live, so I suggest browsing the Asian markets in your neighbourhood and picking up samples of fruits, vegetables and even herbs that you have never dared to use. Taste each of them and try to decide whether their texture and flavour would be good in a tomato salad – some crunchy, some juicy, some soft, some sweet, some sour, some neutral; a little bitterness never hurts. Select your favourite ones and combine them using the recipe here.

truffle-steamed coral trout with grilled watermelon salad, purple carrot purée and pomegranate-torch ginger coulis

ABOUT THE RECIPE: This is one of those recipes that still charms me after all these years as a chef. For a long time, I have been working on marrying the subtle flavours of highly prized Western ingredients (such as truffles) with the flavours of Indonesia. This recipe is a good example of what we have been able to achieve. The exotic combination of truffles, torch ginger and pomegranate conspires to produce a truly tantalising dish, one that is truly worth the time and effort we've put into its creation. There are many such heavenly marriages made at Mozaic, but you'll have to come to our restaurant to try them all ...

PORTION: Serves 4 as an appetiser or 2 as a main course **DIFFICULTY LEVEL:**

INGREDIENTS

Pata Negra
8 slices pata negra ham, thinly sliced

Fish
320 g coral trout fillet, 8 x 40 g or 4 x 80 g pieces
2 tbsp truffle oil
salt and white pepper, to taste
16 slices black truffle
sea salt, to taste

Watermelon Salad
200 g watermelon, skin on, cut into 1½ cm slices
40 pomegranate seeds
2 tbsp truffle oil
2 tsp chives, chopped
salt and white pepper, to taste

Purple Carrot Purée
80 g purple carrots, peeled and chopped
80 ml fresh pomegranate juice
15 g butter
salt and white pepper, to taste

Coulis
500 ml fresh pomegranate juice
1 torch ginger flower, finely chopped

Garnish
4 fresh herb sprigs of your choice

METHOD

For the pata negra, preheat the oven to 160°C. Set aside 4 slices for later use. The remaining 4 slices are to be made into crispy pata negra. Line a baking tray with a silicone mat or baking paper and place the ham slices on it. Lay another silicone mat on top of the ham. Bake for 15–18 minutes, or until dry and crisp. Allow to cool to room temperature and store in an airtight container.

To marinate the fish, season the pieces of coral trout with half the truffle oil, salt and pepper. Place 2 black truffle slices on top of each piece of fish and wrap them individually with cling film. Refrigerate.

For the salad, char-grill one side of the watermelon on a very hot grill for few seconds, or until there are dark, criss-cross grill marks on the fruit (don't grill the other side). Chill immediately in the refrigerator to stop the cooking process (the watermelon must remain crunchy). When cold, cut it into cubes and set aside at room temperature.

To make the purple carrot purée, simmer the carrots in pomegranate juice with the butter and a little salt, until the carrots are tender. Blend everything into a smooth purée in a processor and strain. Adjust the texture of the purée with a little pomegranate juice, so it's nice and smooth. Season to taste with salt and pepper, then set aside.

For the coulis, boil the pomegranate juice and the ginger flower until it has reduced to approximately 60 ml, and its consistency is suitable for plate decorating. Strain and set aside.

To cook the fish, steam the trout in the cling film until it's cooked rare (approximately 4–5 minutes for 40 g pieces and 7–8 minutes for 80 g pieces). Meanwhile, assemble the watermelon salad by tossing the grilled watermelon cubes and pomegranate seeds with the truffle oil, chives, salt and pepper to taste. Drizzle each plate with the coulis, and arrange the salad and 2 small scoops, or quenelles, of purple carrot purée on each plate. Remove the cling film from the fish, then season it with sea salt and the remaining truffle oil. Arrange 2 pieces of fish on each plate. Garnish with 1 slice of fresh and 1 slice of crispy pata negra ham, and fresh herb sprigs.

TIP

At Mozaic, we make our own truffle oil. We fill a jar with truffles, cover it to the brim with salad oil, seal the jar, and place the jar in the freezer for 2–3 weeks before using the oil.

TEMPEH

Indonesian/Balinese: *tempé*
English: tempeh

FOOD CHARACTER

Tempeh is fermented soyabean cake made with whole soyabeans, which give it a stronger and more textured body than tofu. Its flavour is mild and nut-like, evocative of mushrooms, and becomes more pronounced when fried. Tempeh absorbs flavours well and is a very versatile food. Its complete protein content makes tempeh a popular meat substitute, with the added nutritional value of soyabeans.

PHYSICALS

Tempeh is made by soaking and hulling soyabeans, and then boiling them until partially cooked. A culturing agent (*Rhizopus oligosporus*) is introduced, allowing the mixture to ferment for 24 to 36 hours at 30°C – the ambient temperature of Java, where tempeh originated. A soft white blanket of mycelia forms around the beans, binding it into a solid cake. It's cut into pieces and, in Indonesia, is traditionally wrapped in banana leaf for sale.

LOCAL USE

Tempeh is a staple food in Bali, Java and parts of Southeast Asia. It's most commonly sliced, soaked briefly in salted water and then deep fried.
It can also be cut into matchsticks and fried with sweet soya sauce and raw peanuts, or steamed in banana leaf parcels with coconut milk and spices.
A popular dish in Java is *tempé bacem*, where it's simmered in coconut milk, spices and palm sugar, then lightly fried.

NOTES FROM CHEF SALANS

Tempeh is one of those magical ingredients. I fell in love with it the first time I ate it and I'm still crazy about it today. We eat it at home almost every day. My wife tells me that most Indonesians would laugh at me because for them, tempeh is a poor man's food – the first thing an Indonesian would do if he rose in society would be to remove tempeh from his diet. But I'm not Indonesian: I could never give up tempeh.

Selecting the ingredient: In Indonesia, tempeh comes in many forms: wrapped in a banana leaf, in cling film, or without wrapping; and in shades of white, light brown, or blackened; each variation of tempeh has a specific use. The blackened tempeh, for instance, is specifically used for frying. Fresh tempeh should be warm to the touch as the enzymes are still active and release heat. The tempeh should be about 80 percent whole beans and 20 percent mycelia, the fermentation that appears as a white cotton-like substance. A slight ammoniac smell in fresh tempeh is normal. Whenever possible, buy fresh tempeh and freeze it yourself just before use to make it easier to handle. Avoid pre-frozen tempeh as it won't taste as good.

How to prepare it: Traditionally, tempeh is fried, stir-fried, stewed, grilled or baked. It's usually marinated in aromatics before being cooked. In the recipes that follow, tempeh is not used in the traditional Indonesian way. We either freeze tempeh and grate it, or deep fry it until crispy.

Substitutes: There is no substitute for tempeh when used in our recipes, but the good news is that tempeh is commonly found in health food stores or large supermarkets, sold either chilled or frozen.

OPPOSITE Soyabeans are boiled then fermented to make tempeh, which is produced as a cottage industry in Indonesia.
THIS PAGE Tempeh cakes after fermentation in their white blanket of mycelia.

tempeh-crusted king snapper with yellow bell pepper sauce and asian greens

ABOUT THE RECIPE: This dish showcases the unique characteristics of tempeh – specifically, its delectably nutty flavour and crunchy texture. The flavour of tempeh is quite understated on its own, but when paired with a white fish, its distinctive taste shines through and adds a delicious crunch to the fish. The zesty Balinese lemongrass relish that accompanies this dish is the perfect foil for the tempeh-crusted fish, resulting in a sensational dish that your dinner guests will talk about for days.

PORTION: Serves 6 as an appetiser or 3 as a main course **DIFFICULTY LEVEL:**

INGREDIENTS

Bell Pepper Sauce
5 g butter
1 tbsp shallots, chopped
3 cloves garlic, roasted, see Techniques (page 140)
2½ yellow bell peppers, roasted and peeled, see Techniques (page 140)
50–60 ml chicken stock, see Techniques (page 140)
2 kaffir lime leaves, bruised
salt and white pepper, to taste

Lemongrass Relish
¼ tsp shrimp paste, toasted
¼ tsp salt
3 tbsp shallots, finely sliced
2 tbsp lemongrass, finely sliced
1 tbsp coconut oil
3 tbsp Lombok chillies (or red chillies), finely sliced
1 lemo leaf (or any edible lime leaf), finely sliced
½ lemo lime (or any fragrant lime)
salt, to taste

Fish
480 g king snapper fillets, 6 x 80 g or 3 x 160 g portions
60 g fresh tempeh (freeze for 6 hours before use)
salt and white pepper, to taste
1 tbsp salad oil
1 tbsp shallots, chopped
2 pinches thyme leaves
10 g butter, unsalted
sea salt, to taste

Asian Greens
1 tbsp sesame oil
1 tbsp salad oil
1 tbsp ginger, julienned
1 tbsp garlic, finely sliced
2 tsp white sesame seeds
100 g yellow bell peppers, roasted, peeled and diced into 1 x 1 cm cubes
100 g red bell peppers, roasted, peeled and diced into 1 x 1 cm cubes
200 g bok choy, stems cut into batonnets, then blanched until al dente; leaves sliced raw
50 g edamame beans, blanched and peeled
50 g baby corn, cut in segments and blanched
2 tbsp soya sauce
1 tbsp chives, sliced
salt and white pepper, to taste

Garnish
6 fresh herb sprigs of your choice

METHOD

To make the sauce, melt the butter in a pan over medium heat. Add the shallots and garlic. Sauté until the shallots turn translucent. Add the bell peppers and chicken stock, and bring to the boil. Remove from the heat, and process in a blender until smooth. Strain and pour the sauce back into the pan. Bring to the boil again and add the lime leaves. Take off the heat, set aside and allow it to infuse; don't remove the lime leaves as you want to extract as much flavour as you can from the leaves. Season to taste with salt and pepper, and set aside.

For the relish, crumble the shrimp paste and salt together in a bowl. Please note: these steps must be followed precisely in order to achieve the correct balance of flavours. Add the shallots, lemongrass and coconut oil. Combine for a minute using your fingers in a light rubbing motion. Add the chilli and mix well by hand for another minute. Add the lime leaf and mix for another 30 seconds. Then squeeze in the juice of the half lime and throw the entire lime half into the mixture. Do a final toss and adjust the seasoning. Set aside.

Next, prepare the fish crust. Grate the frozen tempeh and coat one side of the fish fillets with the grated tempeh, to form a 3 mm crust. Season the fish with salt and pepper on both sides. Heat the oil in a pan until lightly smoking. Place the fillets, tempeh side down, into the oil. Sear the tempeh until it's golden-brown and no longer sticks to the bottom of the pan. Turn the fillets over, cooking them until they are done to your liking (at Mozaic we serve our fish rare). Just before the fish is done, add the butter, shallots and thyme, and baste the fish with the melted butter. Remove from the pan and drain on paper towels. Season with sea salt.

To stir-fry the Asian greens, heat the salad oil and half the sesame oil in a sauté pan or wok. Add the ginger and garlic, stir-frying until they are lightly browned. Add the sesame seeds and brown them lightly. Add all the vegetables and mix well. Add the soya sauce, and cover the pan with a lid for a minute or until the vegetables have wilted. Season to taste with salt and pepper. Add the chives and remaining sesame oil, and give the greens a final toss. Dish them out immediately, leaving the sauce behind in the wok. Raise the heat and reduce the sauce until it's quite thick.

To serve, make a circle of the yellow bell pepper sauce in the centre of each plate. Pile some vegetables in the centre of each circle. Drizzle the vegetable sauce around the plate. Top the vegetables with a piece of fish and a spoonful of the lemongrass relish. Garnish with a fresh herb sprig and serve immediately.

TIP

Be careful when searing the fish on its tempeh-crusted side. The tempeh has a tendency to fall apart and stick to the pan, so make sure the oil is just starting to smoke before you put the fish in. Also, avoid moving the fish around the pan until the tempeh has turned a nice golden-brown and doesn't stick to the pan anymore. Don't overcook tempeh as it will develop a bitter flavour.

BLACK RICE

(*Oryza sativa* L. *indica*)
Indonesian: *Ketan hitam* (*beras hitam*)
Balinese: *injin*
Also known as: Forbidden Rice (brand name)

FOOD CHARACTER

This is a black variety of glutinous rice that is aromatic and nutty, with a chewy al dente texture.

PHYSICALS

When cooked, the colour becomes a deep burgundy purple. The anthocyanin pigments that cause this (which are also found in blueberries) have significant antioxidant and anti-inflammatory properties, causing some to label black rice a "superfood". The rice is sometimes called purple sticky rice because, as mentioned above, it's not truly black but a very dark purple, which becomes more obvious when cooked.

LOCAL USE

Several varieties of black rice are grown in Indonesia. In Bali, black rice is often mixed with glutinous rice (*ketan*) to make black rice pudding (*bubur injin*). Served with coconut milk, it's a popular dessert in restaurants catering to tourists. It's also used to make *tapé*, a sweet fermented rice snack. Because of its colour, which is associated with the Hindu deity Vishnu and the cardinal point north, it has been adopted as an ingredient in offerings.

NOTES FROM CHEF SALANS

Several of my recipes use black rice as a substitute for flour in order to showcase its exceptional colour and aroma. In the Black Rice Bread recipe (see page 58), it replaces wheat flour and in the light biscuit known as Tuile (see page 125), it's a substitute for rice flour. In a later recipe featuring durian (see page 138), we demonstrate the qualities fermented black rice brings to a sweet dish.

Selecting the ingredient: Choose rice that has full grains rather than broken ones. The black rice we get in Bali often comes uncleaned, that is, with a lot of stones and foreign particles. If you can't find pre-cleaned rice, you will have to clean it yourself, and this can be quite painstaking.

How to prepare it: Pick out the stones and grit, then soak the rice for a few hours in a large amount of water to allow foreign particles to rise to the surface. This can be time-consuming, but the result is well worth it. Because the rice has been pre-soaked, the cooking time will be reduced, as will the amount of water needed to cook the rice, so take this into consideration.

Substitutes: There is no substitute for black rice other than trying to find the branded Forbidden Rice.

OPPOSITE Black rice on the stalk, ready for harvest.
THIS PAGE Husked black rice as one would find it in a Balinese market.

black rice bread

ABOUT THE RECIPE: Here is another magical recipe that exemplifies Mozaic's unique cuisine. Black rice, an unusual ingredient in the West, is very common in Southeast Asia. It's most often used in desserts – my favourite is *bubur injin* or black rice porridge with lashings of thick coconut cream. I added candlenuts to this savoury bread recipe for texture and the result was stunning. Baked in loaves and sliced, it makes a great bread for sandwiches.

*Elements of this recipe should be prepared 1 day in advance.

PORTION: 30 rolls of 40 g each   DIFFICULTY LEVEL: 1 of 3

INGREDIENTS

150 g black rice, uncooked
1 pandan leaf
480 g white bread flour
approx 1.75 litres water
2 tsp cocoa powder
2 tsp salt
2 tbsp instant yeast
50 g candlenuts, boiled and chopped (use macadamia nuts if unavailable)

METHOD

Start the bread the day before. Place the rice in a bowl, cover with cold water and soak for 2 hours. Remove any seeds or grit that float to the surface.

Drain the rice and put it in a saucepan with the pandan leaf and 1 litre of cold water. Bring the contents to the boil over medium heat, stirring continuously. Once the water has been absorbed, add enough water so that it covers the rice by approximately 1 cm. Continue stirring the rice to ensure it doesn't stick. Repeat this process, adding water and stirring, until the rice is cooked al dente. Don't add any more water and continue cooking until all the water has been absorbed. The rice should be cooked until it's fairly dry, with a porridge-like consistency, but it should still have a little "bite". Turn off the heat and cool the rice to room temperature. Refrigerate.

On the day of preparation, preheat the oven to 200°C. Place the chilled black rice (with the pandan leaf removed), flour, cocoa and salt in a mixer with a dough-hook attachment. Mix on low speed for 1 minute, then slowly add the yeast. The consistency of the dough shouldn't be too wet or too dry, so add small amounts of flour or water as needed. Mix on a low speed for 5–7 minutes until a smooth dough has formed and it no longer sticks to the bowl. Then mix on medium speed for approximately 1 minute until the dough becomes elastic. Add the candlenuts and mix for another 30 seconds.

Place the dough on a floured surface and flatten it with your hands so that it's approximately 4 cm high. Using a knife or a dough cutter, cut out pieces of approximately 40 gm and roll the dough into round balls. Set aside to proof until the dough is roughly twice its original size. Bake for 15 minutes. Serve with semi-salted butter.

The bread can be stored in an airtight container for later use, but should be heated in a medium to hot oven (not a microwave) until crispy on the outside before serving.

TIP

Successful breadmaking takes some experience, so I advise practising with a regular bread recipe before trying this out. Pay special attention when cooking the black rice. If undercooked, the rice will be so hard after the bread is baked that it could chip your teeth. If overcooked, the rice will turn to mush and "disappear". When made correctly, the bread will have a nice "bite" to it. Don't be alarmed at the amount of yeast used in this recipe. Because of the dense nature of the rice, more yeast is required in order to make the dough rise sufficiently.

mandarin sorbet with bubur injin and black rice crisps

ABOUT THE RECIPE: *Bubur injin* is a traditional Indonesian porridge made from local black rice. There is nothing like it. It looks beautiful, tastes amazing and is the ultimate comfort food. It reminds me a little of my mother's porridge, except that it's more exotic and appealing. There was no way I'd leave its special flavour out of my menu. But we needed to pair this porridge with another prominent flavour. Something powerful, yet not overpowering. Through trial and error, we created a sorbet made with mandarins and their skins. On its own, it's an extremely strong sorbet with a pronounced rind flavour. When the sorbet is paired with black rice porridge, something magical happens – the balance becomes simply perfect.

PORTION: Serves 10 **DIFFICULTY LEVEL:** 🍴🍴🍴

INGREDIENTS

Sorbet
170 g imperial mandarins
185 g liquid glucose
70 g sugar
1 leaf gelatine, pre-soaked
350 ml orange juice
100 ml lime juice

Black Rice Porridge
100 g black rice, uncooked
approx 1 litre fresh coconut milk
2 pandan leaves
1 pinch salt
75 g coconut palm sugar

Crisps
120 g Black Rice Porridge (recipe above)
2½ tbsp glutinous rice flour
1 tbsp cocoa powder
3½ tbsp white sugar

Candied Orange Peel
2 oranges, skin only
100 g sugar
100 g (not ml) water

Garnishes
200 ml cream, whipped
10 fresh herb sprigs of your choice

Special Equipment
ice cream machine

METHOD

To make the sorbet, peel the skin from the mandarins and set aside the peeled fruit. Place the skins in a saucepan with cold water and bring to the boil. Strain and rinse well under cold water. Repeat this process 4 times. Meanwhile, juice the peeled mandarins. Process the blanched mandarin skins in a blender with the mandarin juice until smooth. Strain. Place the mixture in a saucepan with the glucose and sugar, and simmer over medium heat until the liquid is reduced by half. Strain, then add the gelatine and stir until it dissolves. Add the orange and lime juice and stir well. Chill the mixture in the refrigerator, then churn in an ice cream machine until the sorbet hardens. Transfer to a plastic container and freeze.

Before making the porridge, place the rice in a bowl, cover it with cold water and soak for 2 hours. Remove any seeds or grit that float to the surface. Put the black rice, coconut milk, pandan leaves and salt in a saucepan, and simmer over low heat. Stir regularly to ensure the rice doesn't stick to the bottom of the pan and burn. Simmer until the rice is tender but not completely soft (this should take 45–60 minutes). Add sugar and stir until it has dissolved. Set aside.

For the crisps, preheat the oven to 110°C. Blend all the ingredients in a food processor until smooth. Strain. Place spoonfuls of batter on a non-stick mat or baking paper and spread each one with a spoon into circles that are 1 mm thick and 7–8 cm in diameter. Bake for 15 minutes. Flip the crisps and bake for 1 hour, or until crispy. Remove from the oven and allow them to cool. Store in an airtight container.

To prepare the candied orange peel, cut the skin (ie, zest and white pith) off the oranges with a sharp knife and set aside the peeled fruit for later use. Cover the skins with water and bring to the boil. Strain and rinse thoroughly. Repeat this process 4 more times. Place the blanched skin, sugar and water in a saucepan over very low heat, and gently simmer until a thick syrup forms. Taste the skin; it should be tender and sweet. If not, add a little water and continue cooking. Remove from the heat and allow it to cool to room temperature. Remove the skins from the syrup and and cut them into ½ cm wide strips.

To assemble, reheat the porridge in a saucepan. Its consistency should be suitable for plate decorating. Drizzle patterns on the plates with the porridge. Place 2 small scoops, or quenelles, of whipped cream on each plate, and top with strips of candied orange peel. Segment the 2 peeled oranges and arrange 2 segments close together in the centre of the plate. Place a quenelle of sorbet on top of the orange segments. Garnish the sorbet with black rice crisps and a fresh herb sprig. Serve immediately.

TIPS

Wheat flour-based biscuits and crisps lose their crunch quickly in places with high humidity. To prevent them from going soggy and limp, try using rice flour – a secret I discovered while munching on crispy local pastries at night markets in Bali.

For more information on simple syrups and how to make sorbet if you don't have an ice cream machine, see Techniques (page 140).

KLUWEK NUT

Pangium edule (*Flacourtiaceae* or *Violales*)
Indonesian: *kluwek* (*kluwak*, *kluak*)
Balinese: *pangi*
Malay: *kepayang*

FOOD CHARACTER

This large, hard-shelled exotic nut grows wild in the mangrove swamps of Indonesia and Malaysia. After processing, the paste-like nut takes on a rich, smoky, almond-like flavour and oily texture. In cooking, it adds an intense, almost black colour to any dish you cook.

PHYSICALS

The *pangi* or *kepayang* tree grows up to 60 metres high, and it takes 10–15 years to bear fruit. For this reason, the kluwek nut, which appears seasonally from May to August, is harvested wild. The raw fruit and seeds contain the water-soluble toxin, hydrogen cyanide. Fortunately, kluwek nuts sold in markets would already have been processed to make them safe for consumption. The toxins are removed by boiling the nuts, wrapping them in ash and banana leaves, and burying the mixture in earth for 40 days. This process changes the nut from a creamy white to almost black.

LOCAL USE

Kluwek is an important ingredient in *rawon*, a classic Javanese beef curry, to which it lends its very dark colour. In Bali, it's used in the condiment *sambal pangi* (*sambal kluwek*) and in offerings. In Indonesia, kluwek is found in its shell in local markets, but it is also packaged and sold already hulled.

NOTES FROM CHEF SALANS

Kluwek is an extremely obscure ingredient outside of Indonesia, Malaysia and Singapore. Its pungent, smoky aroma with hints of underwood reminds me of forest mushrooms. Although in the following recipes I have kept the use of kluwek to the basics, I foresee great potential in pairing kluwek with ingredients like black truffle and chocolate. Kluwek could be a star ingredient, if not for its relative scarcity.

Selecting the ingredient: The shell of the kluwek nut should have a nice dark colour. As it ages, the shell tends to become cloudy white, and the inner nut dries out and turns mouldy. The nut of a kluwek with a whitened shell will be much less fragrant. A second test is to shake the nut. If you feel something moving inside, the nut is probably full and moist. If there is no movement, the nut has probably dried up. When unshelled, the kluwek nut should be large, plump and moist, and of a uniformly dark-brown colour.

How to prepare it: As an added safeguard, kluwek should be pre-boiled to make it completely safe. Place the shelled nuts in a saucepan and add water until the nuts are just covered. Bring the water quickly to the boil. Strain the nut and rinse it. If the nut paste is a bit dried out, you can simmer it for several minutes to make it softer and easier to use.

Substitutes: Unfortunately, there is no substitute for kluwek nuts. There is nothing in the Western world that comes close to it.

OPPOSITE Kluwek nuts in their hulls, opened and shelled.
THIS PAGE *Sambal kluwek* is a popular Indonesian condiment made from the kluwek nut.

steamed squab and wilted greens in a kluwek broth with fresh galangal

ABOUT THE RECIPE: I still remember the first time I tasted *rawon*. It was another of those many culinary discoveries I make while eating al fresco in Indonesia, completely clueless about what is being served to me at the roadside *warung* (casual food stall). On this particular day, I was served *rawon*, a spicy black broth with pieces of beef floating in it and a side of rice. It was so simple – just beef cooked with kluwek nut – yet it tasted so wonderful. The aroma of the kluwek was reminiscent of that of the woods where I picked mushrooms as a child in France, yet it had hints of smokiness, as if the meat had been smoked. But no, all the flavour came from the unassuming black nut. In the following recipe, we re-interpret the kluwek broth of the traditional *rawon*. We wanted to pair kluwek with ingredients that enhance its natural forest aromas, which I hope will take you back to your childhood – if you've ever lived in France, that is.

PORTION: Serves 4 as an appetiser or 2 as a main course **DIFFICULTY LEVEL:**

INGREDIENTS

Squab Stock
300 g bones and wings from whole squab, cleaned
3 tbsp salad oil
½ medium onion, diced
½ medium carrot, peeled and diced
½ stick celery, diced
6 cm leek, sliced
1 pinch salt
700 ml water
3 cloves garlic, crushed
1 salam leaf
6 black peppercorns
1 sprig thyme

Kluwek Broth
1 kluwek nut, paste only, crumbled
Squab Stock (recipe above)
1 tsp coriander seeds, dry roasted
2 kaffir lime leaves, sliced
4 slices galangal, 2 mm thick
1 clove garlic, sliced
24 coriander leaves, sliced
100 g bangkuang (also called yam bean or jicama), scooped with a melon baller
salt, to taste

Squab
2 squab, 240 g each
4 kaffir lime leaves
salt and white pepper, to taste
kaffir lime salt, to taste, see Techniques (page 140)
1 tbsp salad oil

Vegetables
15 g butter, unsalted
200 g oyster mushrooms, sliced
2 tbsp shallots, finely chopped
½ tsp thyme leaves
6 cloves garlic, roasted, see Techniques (page 140)
200 g baby kale, halved
3 tbsp chicken stock, see Techniques (page 140)
salt and white pepper, to taste

Garnishes
12 strips galangal, julienned
4 fresh herb sprigs of your choice

METHOD

To prepare the squab, remove the breasts by cutting them away from the breastbones with a sharp knife. Carefully pull the legs backward to snap the joint, then cut around the joint to remove them. Set aside. Keep the remaining pieces of the bird, including the bones and wings, for the squab stock. Season each breast to taste, then wrap in cling film with 1 lime leaf. Refrigerate.

To make the stock, sear the squab bones and wings with 2 tbsp of oil over medium to high heat until the bones are dark brown but not burnt. Remove the bones from the pan and discard the oil. Turn the heat to low, add another tbsp of oil and gently fry the onion, carrot, celery and leek with a pinch of salt. When the vegetables become translucent, put the browned squab bones and wings back into the pan. Add the remaining ingredients, including the water, and bring to the boil, then immediately reduce the heat so the stock is gently simmering. Simmer until the liquid has reduced by half. Using a spoon, skim off any impurities, foam or oil that rise to the surface. Remove from the heat and allow it to rest for 30 minutes before straining.

Place the kluwek nut paste in a saucepan, cover with cold water and bring to the boil. Simmer for 1 minute, then strain. Bring the squab stock to the boil and add the nut paste, coriander seeds, lime leaves, galangal and garlic, then remove from the heat, cover and allow to infuse for 20 minutes. Adjust the seasoning and strain.

Steam the squab breasts in their cling film for 6–7 minutes, or until they are cooked rare to medium-rare (squab is best served medium-rare to avoid making it tough). Meanwhile, season the squab legs with salt and pepper, and sear them in salad oil until they are cooked through.

Meanwhile, add the bangkuang and coriander leaves to the squab stock and reheat.

To prepare the vegetables, sauté the mushrooms in butter until they are lightly coloured. Add the shallots, garlic and thyme. Add the baby kale and give it a quick stir. Immediately add the stock, then remove the pan from the heat and cover. Once the kale has wilted (approximately 1 minute), remove the lid, season with salt and pepper, and use immediately.

When everything is cooked and the stock is hot, unwrap the steamed squab and remove the lime leaf. Season the breasts and legs with kaffir lime salt.

To assemble, place some vegetables in the centre of each bowl. Pour the stock over the vegetables, then top with a squab breast and leg. Garnish with the galangal and a fresh herb sprig. Serve immediately.

TIP

The most important part of this recipe is the stock. If you make a good stock the dish will be great, so follow the directions to the letter. Towards the end of the cooking time, make sure you leave a little fat in the stock when you are skimming any impurities from the surface; it will add so much flavour.

grilled thunderfish with kluwek-black olive sauce, sambal kluwek and bell peppers

ABOUT THE RECIPE: After my first experience of eating Indonesian *rawon*, or "black soup", at a roadside *warung*, I immediately asked my staff in Mozaic to show me how to use the kluwek nut, which gives the soup its distinctive colour. It was then that I discovered some wonderful ways of incorporating kluwek into my dishes. In this fish recipe we include a traditional Balinese condiment called *sambal kluwek*. It's amazing on its own, but can also be infused into preparations or blended into sauces, such as the black olive sauce found in this recipe. A fish grilled simply with natural wood really complements the smoky flavour of the kluwek nut.

PORTION: Serves 4 as an appetiser or 2 as a main course

DIFFICULTY LEVEL:

INGREDIENTS

Sambal Kluwek

3 kluwek nuts, paste extracted
¼ tsp toasted shrimp paste
¼ tsp salt
3 shallots, finely sliced
1 tbsp coconut oil
2 large Lombok chillies (or red chillies), finely sliced
2 lemo lime leaves (or any edible lime leaf), finely sliced
½ lemo lime (or any fragrant lime)
salt, to taste

Black Olive Sauce

2 tbsp Sambal Kluwek (recipe above)
75 g black olives, pitted and rinsed
75 ml fish stock
1½ tbsp extra virgin olive oil
salt and white pepper, to taste

Bell Peppers

1 yellow bell pepper, top cut off and seeds removed
1 red bell pepper, top cut off and seeds removed
15 g butter, unsalted
1 tbsp shallots, finely chopped
8 cloves garlic, roasted, see Techniques (page 140)
1 pinch thyme leaves
1 tbsp chicken stock, see Techniques (page 140)
salt and pepper, to taste

Fish

320 g thunderfish fillet, 4 x 80 g or 2 x 160 g
salt and white pepper, to taste
2 tbsp salad oil

Garnish

4 fresh herb sprigs of your choice

METHOD

To make the sambal kluwek, put the shelled nut paste in a pan, cover with cold water and bring to the boil. Simmer for 1 minute, then strain. Crumble the shrimp paste and salt together in a bowl. Please note: the following steps must be followed precisely in order to achieve the correct balance of flavours. Add the shallots and half the coconut oil and, using your fingers in a light rubbing motion, combine the ingredients for 1 minute. Add the chillies and combine in the same manner for 1 minute, adding the remaining coconut oil at this point. Repeat this process with the lime leaf, followed by the kluwek nut paste. Finally, squeeze in the juice of the lime, throwing the entire lime half into the mixture as well. Give the ingredients a final toss and adjust the seasoning. Set aside.

To make the sauce, place the sambal kluwek, black olives and fish stock in a saucepan. Bring to the boil, then take off the heat. Blend until smooth, gradually incorporating the olive oil. Strain into a saucepan, season with salt and pepper and set aside.

To prepare the bell peppers, roast and peel the peppers, then cut them into 1 x 1 cm squares. In a saucepan over low heat, cook the shallots in the butter until they are translucent. Add the garlic, thyme and bell peppers. Mix well and adjust the seasoning. Add the chicken stock and stir to emulsify the butter into the sauce.

To cook the fish, heat a grill or grill pan to medium heat. Place the oil, salt and pepper on a plate or tray, and roll the fish in the mixture, ensuring it's well coated. Place the fish on the hot grill and allow it to sear for 1–2 minutes. Turn the fish 90° and allow to sear for another 1–2 minutes so it develops nice criss-cross grill marks. Move the fish over to the side of the grill away from the high heat and allow it to cook slowly (an 80 g portion of fish won't need to be flipped, provided it finishes cooking on low heat at the side of the grill. If you are serving a larger piece of fish, feel free to flip it if it requires further cooking). Once the fish is cooked, remove it from the grill and drain on paper towels.

To serve, make a circle of sauce in the centre of each preheated plate or bowl. Reheat the vegetables in a saucepan and spoon some into the centre of the sauce. Place the fish on top of the vegetables. Sprinkle with sea salt, top with some sambal kluwek and a fresh herb sprig, and serve immediately.

TIP

The kluwek-black olive sauce is also a great base for a dressing. Mix it with a little more olive or salad oil and lemon juice, and toss it with a salad. It gives great results.

CURRY LEAF

Murraya koenigii (L.) Sprenge (*Rutaceae*)
Indonesian: *daun kari*
Also known as: sweet neem leaves

FOOD CHARACTER

These small, delicate, pointy green leaves have a tangy aroma reminiscent of citrus and anise. Although they aren't found in mixed curry spices, small quantities of fresh curry leaves are used in Indian curries and stews, where they are allowed to float freely. Some techniques call for curry leaves to be toasted or quickly fried in hot oil to release their surprising flavour, before adding them to the curry.

PHYSICALS

The pretty, shrub-like curry tree is native to India and found throughout Southeast Asia wherever there has been a history of Indian influence (except, oddly, for Bali, where Indian influence came via Java). The leaves are clusters of 24 feathery leaflets. The white flowers and sweet, shiny black fruits are edible. However, the seeds are toxic.

LOCAL USES

The plant grows abundantly in Java, and is used in Javanese cuisine in dishes such as *gulai*, or lamb stew. Because of its strong flavour, curry leaves are most often used in meat dishes.

NOTES FROM CHEF SALANS

In the following recipes, we show not only how to use fresh curry leaves in the traditional manner (infused in a preparation), but also how to incorporate them in more unusual ways, such as frying them in a butter sauce or using them to roast or smoke a product. I also discovered that the plant's flowers and fruit taste as good as the leaves, and we have developed a lot of recipes with them. Please note that the seeds are toxic and should be removed from the fruit.

Selecting the ingredient: Try to get fresh curry leaves. They are often available in Indian food stores that sell fresh produce. The leaves should be harvested as a branch and picked just before use. Choose leaves that are fresh with no bruising and are a vibrant dark green.

How to prepare it: Curry leaves require no preparation. They can be infused in a liquid and removed, or simply left in the preparation for a stronger flavour. They are also great when fried or added to a butter sauce, and are wonderful in sweet dishes. To preserve the fresh leaves, wrap them in a dry cloth and refrigerate them in a ziplock bag. They should keep for one to two weeks. If you want to keep them longer, freeze them separately, not as a bundle. Once they are frozen, stack them together.

Substitutes: Curry leaves are also available frozen or dried from some Asian food stores, but the quantity may need adjustment, as their aroma won't be as strong as fresh leaves.

OPPOSITE Delicate curry leaves on the bush.
THIS PAGE Fresh curry leaves sautéed in butter add a lovely flavour to preparations.

curry leaf-steamed bass, burnt cauliflower, trumpet mushrooms and curry meunière

ABOUT THE RECIPE: Before we married, my wife would meet me after work late at night for a bite. She once took me to a literal hole in the wall and ordered a dish of fatty meat in an oily yellow broth with leaves floating on the surface. It looked thoroughly unappetising, but when I closed my eyes and tasted it – wow! That was my first experience of curry leaves. As they are grown in Java, my wife's family would send a big box over every few months. Later, I decided to try growing them. Numerous dead plants later, I found out that nine out of 10 plants die due to the climate and soil in Bali. Finally, we hit that lucky 10th plant and, voilà! The restaurant now has a regular supply for the recipes I've developed using curry leaves.

PORTION: Serves 6 as an appetiser or 3 as a main course **DIFFICULTY LEVEL:**

INGREDIENTS

Cauliflower Purée
200 g cauliflower, cut into florets
100 ml milk
100 ml water
1 salam leaf
1 sprig thyme
1 tbsp extra virgin walnut oil
salt, to taste

Curry Foam
2 tsp galangal, chopped
1 tsp ginger, chopped
2 tsp shallots, chopped
½ clove garlic, crushed
1 tsp Madras curry powder
10 fresh curry leaves
300 ml fish stock
½ stalk lemongrass, bruised
1 salam leaf
5 threads saffron
2 kaffir lime leaves
¼ tsp soya lecithin powder (or more if needed); you can also use unsalted butter

Mushrooms
2 tbsp salad oil
15 g butter, unsalted
300 g black trumpet mushrooms
2 tbsp shallots, chopped
1 pinch thyme leaves
salt and pepper, to taste
50 ml chicken stock, see Techniques (page 140)

Fish
480 g black bass fillet, 6 x 80 g or 3 x 160 g portions
6 fresh curry leaves
6 tbsp olive oil
salt and pepper, to taste
sea salt, to taste

Cauliflower
2 tbsp walnut oil
200 g cauliflower, cut into florets
1 tbsp chives, sliced
salt and white pepper, to taste

Meunière Sauce
4 tbsp butter, unsalted
1 tbsp shallots, chopped
1 pinch thyme leaves
8 fresh curry leaves
½ tsp Madras curry powder
1 tbsp flat leaf parsley, chopped
1–2 tbsp lemon juice
salt and white pepper, to taste

Garnish
4 fresh herb sprigs of your choice

METHOD

To make the cauliflower purée, combine the cauliflower, milk, water, salam leaf and thyme in a saucepan and simmer until the cauliflower is tender. Remove the salam leaf and thyme, and strain. Blend the cauliflower in a processor until smooth. Strain again. Season with salt and pepper, then add the walnut oil. Mix well and set aside.

To make the curry foam, sauté the galangal, ginger, shallots and garlic in oil until translucent. Add the curry leaves and curry powder, then deglaze with the fish stock. Add the lemongrass, lime leaves, salam leaf and saffron. Simmer until the liquid has reduced by half. Strain. Add the soya lecithin and blend the liquid with a hand blender to develop a strong foam. You can use 2 tbsp of unsalted butter instead of soya lecithin, but the foam won't rise and hold as well.

To prepare the mushrooms, heat half the oil and half the butter in a pan over medium to high heat. When the butter begins to bubble, add half the mushrooms, allowing them to colour slightly before seasoning with salt and pepper. Add half the shallots and thyme, then remove the pan from the heat so the shallots don't burn. Toss gently, allowing the shallots to cook in the residual heat in the pan. Add half the chicken stock and set aside. Repeat the process with the other half of the ingredients.

To marinate the fish, season the portions with salt and pepper. Wrap each portion individually in cling film with 1 tbsp of olive oil and 1 curry leaf. Refrigerate.

To make the burnt cauliflower, pour the walnut oil in a roasting pan or stainless-steel tray and place it in a hot (220°C plus) oven. When the oil is hot, add the cauliflower florets and allow them to roast until they develop a dark, almost burnt colour on the bottom. Season with salt and pepper, add the chives and mix thoroughly. Although the results aren't quite as good, you can also "burn" the cauliflower on the stove top using salad oil in a frypan. Once it's done, season it with walnut oil, salt and pepper. Use immediately.

To prepare the fish, cook the cling film packets of fish in a steamer or steam oven until the flesh becomes translucent. Depending on the thickness of the fish and the heat of the steamer, this should take 4–5 minutes.

Next, spoon a circle of cauliflower purée onto each plate and place the burnt cauliflower in the centre. Remove the cooked fish from the cling film, throw away the curry leaf and season with sea salt. Place a portion of fish on top of each pile of cauliflower.

Meanwhile, make the meunière sauce. Melt the butter in a pan over medium heat. Allow the butter to bubble for a few minutes. Once it has almost finished bubbling and turns golden, add the shallots, thyme, curry leaves and curry powder. Let the mixture foam up for 15 seconds, then add the parsley. Add the lemon juice 5 seconds later. Season to taste with salt and pepper and immediately drizzle the sauce over the fish.

Top each fish portion with some mushrooms and a few spoonfuls of the curry foam. Garnish each portion with a fresh herb sprig and serve immediately.

TIPS

When choosing your cauliflower, look for one that is very white and has as few spots as possible.

Not every fish is meant to be steamed. Certain fish are better roasted, grilled or seared. Make sure you ask your fishmonger for a fish that is suitable for steaming. We have used black bass due to its pleasant, light taste and availability, but there are dozens of other fish that could also be used.

Meunière sauce has to be made at the last minute as it doesn't keep well and can't be reheated.

slow-roasted lamb with a curry leaf-infused demi-glaçe, eggplant caviar, cardamom reduction and fresh yoghurt

ABOUT THE RECIPE: This dish is a great display of the delicious treasures from the Indonesian *terroir*. Baby lamb from the mountains of Java, fresh curry leaves harvested from my backyard and spices from the islands of Banda in Maluku province. The idea was to use all these great local ingredients and re-create a traditional curry with curry leaves, cardamom and yoghurt. To be sure, there are other elements to a curry but we didn't want to overcomplicate things. Here, the different ingredients complement each other very well and enhance the beautiful flavour of the fresh curry leaf – the star of our dish. I particularly enjoy the technique of roasting lamb over branches and leaves of the curry leaf shrub (a luxury, obviously, if it doesn't grow in your backyard). It's such a great way to impart a smoky, curry flavour to the meat.

PORTION: Serves 10 as an appetiser or 5 as a main course **DIFFICULTY LEVEL:**

INGREDIENTS

Toasted Spices
3 tbsp juniper berries, whole
20 g black peppercorns
4 tbsp almonds, sliced or slivered
2 tsp curry powder
50 g aren palm sugar
50 g coconut palm sugar

Cardamom Reduction
½ tsp cardamom seeds
50 g white sugar
2 tbsp warm water
25 ml white wine vinegar

Eggplant Caviar
500 g eggplant
2 tbsp olive oil
salt and white pepper, to taste
100 ml extra virgin olive oil
1 tbsp garlic, roasted, see Techniques (page 140)

Lamb
1 leg baby lamb, on the bone
salt and white pepper, to taste
2 tbsp salad oil
1 bunch curry leaves, whole branches

Jelly
100 ml milk
1 tsp sugar
4 tsp milk powder
2 tsp plain konnyaku jelly powder (Nutrijell or any other quality brand)

Yoghurt
2 tbsp plain unsweetened yoghurt
½ tsp red wine vinegar
salt and pepper, to taste

Spinach
35 g butter, unsalted
6 cloves garlic, roasted
3 tbsp shallots, chopped
250 g spinach leaves, stems removed
salt and white pepper, to taste

Curry Leaf Sauce
100 ml beef demi-glaçe, see Techniques (page 140)
6 curry leaves
1 clove garlic, crushed
salt and black pepper, to taste

Garnish
6 fresh curry leaves on the stem

METHOD

For the toasted spices, preheat the oven to 160°C. Grind the berries, peppercorns and almonds in a coffee or spice grinder; the texture should be neither too coarse nor too fine. Add the curry powder and both types of sugar, and mix thoroughly. Place the mixture on a baking tray lined with a non-stick mat or baking paper, and bake for approximately 15 minutes; the mixture should start to bubble when it's ready. Remove the tray from the oven and allow it to cool to room temperature. Break the mixture into small pieces and store in an airtight container.

To prepare the cardamom reduction, dry roast the cardamom seeds in a pan over low heat until they are fragrant. Set aside. Stir the sugar in the same pan over medium heat until it melts and caramelises (approximately 5 minutes). Remove from the heat and add the water. Stir until the caramel has dissolved in the water. Allow to cool for a while. Blend the caramel and cardamom seeds until smooth. Thin the mixture with the vinegar.

To prepare the eggplant caviar, preheat the oven to 200°C with a roasting tray inside. Cut the eggplants in half, leaving their peduncles on. Season with 2 tbsp of olive oil, salt and pepper. Put the eggplant halves on the hot roasting tray and roast until they are very soft. Cool to room temperature. Scoop out the flesh, including the brown, roasted parts. Place the flesh in a strainer and allow it to drain in the refrigerator for a minimum of 2 hours. Combine the refrigerated eggplant pulp with 100 ml of extra virgin olive oil and the garlic, and blend in a food processor. Season with salt and pepper. Set aside and reheat prior to serving.

To prepare the baby lamb, line an oven tray with the curry leaf branches. Preheat the oven to 200°C with the tray inside. Meanwhile, season the lamb with salt and pepper. Heat the oil in a pan and sear the lamb on all sides. Place the lamb on the hot tray in the oven, close the door and turn the heat off. Allow the meat to cook in the residual heat for 1–1½ hours. Don't open the oven door during this time.

For the jelly, place all the ingredients in a saucepan over medium heat. Boil for 30 seconds, stirring continuously with a whisk. Pour the liquid into a container; the depth of the liquid should be approximately 1½ cm. Cool to room temperature, then cut the jelly into 1½ x 1½ cm cubes. Set aside.

Stir all the ingredients for the yoghurt gently, taking care it doesn't become too thin and watery.

To prepare the spinach, add the butter to a sauté pan and allow it to brown lightly over medium heat. Add the shallots and garlic. Remove from the heat and add the spinach leaves. Toss quickly, allowing the spinach to wilt. Season to taste with salt and pepper.

To make the curry leaf sauce, bring the demi-glaçe to the boil. Add the curry leaves and garlic, and cover with a lid. Set aside and allow it to infuse for 15 minutes. Season to taste with salt and pepper.

When the lamb is ready, slice it thinly. Divide the meat into 6 portions and arrange the slices on a tray. Season with salt and pepper and reheat the meat in a hot oven. Decorate the pre-warmed plates with the cardamom reduction, yoghurt and a spoonful of the toasted spices. Place 2 cubes of jelly, a small mound of spinach and a spoonful of warmed eggplant caviar on each plate. When the meat is warm and done to your liking (it shouldn't be overcooked), remove it from the oven and arrange the lamb slices over the spinach. Drizzle a spoonful of curry leaf sauce on top of the meat. Garnish with a sprig of curry leaves and serve immediately.

TIP

For more information on making a caramel and roasting garlic, see Techniques (page 140).

PEPPERCORNS

There are many kinds of peppercorns available in Indonesia. The major ones are: andaliman pepper, *Zanthoxylum acanthopodium* (*Rutaceae*), called *intir-intir* in Indonesian and also known as lemon pepper; tabia bun (its Balinese name), *Piper retrofractum Vahl.* (*Piperaceae*), known as *lada panjang* in Indonesian and Indonesian long pepper in English; Java comet tail, *Piper cubeba*, called *kemukus* or *lada jawa* in Indonesia and also known as Java pepper or cubeb; and fresh green, black and white peppercorns, *Piper nigrum* (*Piperaceae*), called *merica* (respectively *hijau*, *hitam* and *putih*) in Indonesian.

FOOD CHARACTER

Andaliman pepper is an aromatic berry with a woody, lemon-like taste, whose fragrance and milder heat make it a striking alternative to conventional black and white pepper. Tabia bun pepper has a hot, slightly sweet and earthy aroma that has been compared to damp hemp rope. The aroma of Java comet tail is somewhat like allspice. Green peppercorns are highly fragrant with an agreeable texture; black pepper brings heat and characteristic aroma; and white pepper, which is slightly hotter, is often preferred in white sauces.

PHYSICALS

The aroma and pungency of andaliman pepper are only in the pericarp (hull); the gritty inner seeds are discarded. Tabia bun is native to Southeast Asia and cultivated mostly in Indonesia and Thailand. The fruit is long and nearly black, with tiny seeds that merge to form a catkin-like rod. Java comet tail has hard, white, oily seeds encased in a wrinkled grey-black hull that has a stem or "tail". *Piper nigrum* – the regular pepper that most cooks use – grows on a climbing vine. Green peppercorns are picked fresh when the berries are still tender. Black pepper is created by drying the hard green berry. White pepper is the hulled seed. The heat of the peppercorn increases at each progressive stage.

LOCAL USE

Andaliman pepper is used among the Batak of Sumatra, as is tabia bun, which is used in Bali and Java in savoury dishes. Java comet tail is used in Indonesia to flavour spirits and cigarettes as well as in cooking, especially in *gulai*, an Indonesian-style curry cooked with chicken, meat or seafood.

NOTES FROM CHEF SALANS

Peppercorns are another example of an ingredient that changes from one Indonesian island to the next. We're lucky to have a lot of fresh peppercorn trees in Bali, so we can pick the ingredient right off the tree. In the following recipes, we showcase three peppercorns available in Bali: fresh green peppercorn, tabia bun and andaliman pepper. Some of the other peppercorns are used in recipes throughout this book.

Selecting the ingredient: Peppercorns are found in many different forms, including fresh, half-dried and fully dried. I prefer the fresh or half-dried versions as they have more of a fresh spice flavour.

How to prepare it: All the peppercorns, except for the fresh green peppercorn and tabia bun, are prepared the same way: crushed or ground and then infused before being discarded, or left in the dish for extra heat. It's recommended that all dried spices (including dried peppercorns) be toasted, baked in the oven or dry roasted over medium heat until they become fragrant. Fresh green peppercorns shouldn't be ground or toasted, they should simply be crushed or used whole. With tabia bun, the pepper itself is the outside shell that protects the seeds within. Crack then toast the pepper to draw out its full aroma, and then grind it if you like. The flavour will be strong.

Substitutes: There is no substitute for tabia bun, but any other exotic peppercorn can be used instead.

OPPOSITE *Top to bottom*: tabia bun, Java comet tail, fresh green peppercorns, dried black peppercorns and white peppercorns.
THIS PAGE *Piper nigrum*, the common pepper, on the vine.

tabia bun-marinated venison with wilted cabbage salad, tenggulun berry-infused red wine reduction and toasted spices

ABOUT THE RECIPE: The tabia bun pepper is unusual because, unlike other peppers, you have to break it open to collect the individual peppercorns hidden inside. This recipe is based on a reinterpretation of the classic French sauce *grand veneur*, where sweet and sour cranberries are used in a peppery sauce. I have omitted the cognac and cream, making the sauce lighter, but infused it with the powerful tabia bun pepper. Due to popular demand, we have also found a way to serve the pepper on the side in the form of a spice mix, for those of our guests who expect heat in our food because we're in Southeast Asia. This recipe uses the confit technique and while it's an invaluable cooking method, one must remember it should only be used for meats that don't require the flavour acquired from caramelisation (achieved when roasting, searing or grilling). Venison is a good example of a meat that is wonderful when confied.

PORTION: Serves 6 as an appetiser or 3 as a main course **DIFFICULTY LEVEL:** ♆♆♆

INGREDIENTS

Cranberries
200 g sugar
200 g (not ml) water
100 g fresh or frozen fresh cranberries

Tenggulun Reduction
300 ml good quality red wine
300 ml port wine
50 g tenggulun berries (optional)
1 pinch salt

Toasted Spices
15 g tabia bun pepper
3 tbsp juniper berries
4 tbsp almonds, sliced or slivered
2 tsp lemon zest, finely grated
50 g aren palm sugar
50 g coconut palm sugar

Tabia Bun Demi-Glaçe
1 tabia bun pepper pod
150 ml beef demi-glaçe, see Techniques (page 140)
1 5-cm sprig rosemary
1 clove garlic
12 poached cranberries
2 tbsp cranberry poaching liquid
1 tbsp red wine vinegar
salt, to taste

Venison
500 g venison loin, cleaned
salt, to taste
1 tabia bun pepper pod, ground, to taste
1 litre salad oil
3–4 sprigs rosemary

Cabbage Salad
150 g red cabbage, finely shredded
2 tbsp fat from cooked foie gras
2 pinches thyme leaves
2 pinches salt
1 tbsp cranberry poaching liquid
1 tbsp red wine vinegar
18 poached cranberries
3–4 chestnuts, roasted and sliced
1 tbsp flat leaf parsley, chopped
sea salt and white pepper, to taste

Garnish
6 fresh herb sprigs of your choice

METHOD

To poach the cranberries, bring the sugar and water to the boil, stirring to dissolve the sugar. Once the sugar has dissolved, add the cranberries and simmer until they are cooked. They should be tender to eat but still hold their shape. Set aside.

For the tenggulun reduction, place all the ingredients in a saucepan and simmer until it has reduced by three-quarters. Strain the liquid, pressing down on the berries to extract all the juice. Return to the heat and reduce the strained sauce until the consistency is suitable for plate decorating.

To prepare the toasted spices, preheat the oven to 160°C. Grind the spices in a spice or coffee mill until the mixture is not too coarse and not too fine (like the texture of dried breadcrumbs). Add the almonds and coarsely grind them. Add the zest and palm sugars, and mix until the ingredients are thoroughly combined. Spread the mixture on a baking tray lined with a non-stick mat or baking paper and bake for approximately 15 minutes (the mixture will start to bubble when it's ready). Remove the tray from the oven and allow to cool to room temperature. When cool, break into small pieces. Store in an airtight container.

To prepare the demi-glaçe, break the tabia bun into several pieces and dry roast them in a pan until they're fragrant. Add the demi-glaçe, bring it to the boil, then add the rosemary and garlic. Remove from the heat, cover and allow to infuse for 15–20 minutes.

Return the pan to the heat, bring the sauce back to the boil and season with salt. Add the cranberry juice and red wine vinegar to taste. The sauce should have a pronounced but pleasant sweet and sour flavour that balances the heat of the pepper. Reduce the sauce until it reaches the right consistency. Note: add the cranberries to the sauce just prior to serving so the fruit is warmed through, but not cooked until mushy.

To cook the venison, preheat the oven to 60°C. Season the venison with salt and ground tabia bun pepper. Place the meat in an ovenproof dish; it should fit snugly. Add enough oil to cover the venison by at least 1 cm. Add the rosemary sprigs to the oil, then place the dish in the oven. After 30 minutes, turn the meat over and cook for another 30 minutes. Then, remove it from the oven, take the venison out of the oil and pat it dry with paper towels.

To make the cabbage salad, put the cabbage, foie gras fat, thyme and regular salt in a mixing bowl. Seal with aluminium foil and place the bowl on top of a pan of gently simmering water. Allow the cabbage to wilt; it should be half-cooked and still al dente (this should take approximately 5 minutes). Season with sea salt, pepper, cranberry poaching liquid and red wine vinegar to taste. Then add the poached cranberries, chestnuts and parsley, and mix well.

To assemble the dish, preheat the oven to 160–180°C. Slice the venison thinly (it should be rare) and fan it out into 6 portions on a roasting tray. Season with salt and pepper, and place the tray in the oven until the meat is done to your liking.

Drizzle each plate with the tenggulun reduction, and arrange the salad and a tbsp of toasted spices on it. Arrange the meat on the plates and pour the hot demi-glaçe over it. Place 2 poached cranberries on each plate, one on each side of the meat. Garnish with a fresh herb sprig and serve immediately.

TIPS

If fat from cooked foie gras isn't available, canned duck fat is a good substitute. Alternatively, olive oil or another form of healthier fat can be used, but the cabbage salad won't have the same rich flavour.

For information on simple syrups and setting very low oven temperatures, see Techniques (page 140).

green peppercorn-chocolate mousse with lime glaze and peppercorn-wine reduction

ABOUT THE RECIPE: Here is another variation of our popular chocolate mousse, where a flavoured jelly is hidden within. This time, we use a peppercorn jelly. It may be difficult to imagine fresh peppercorn and chocolate working well together, but it does. There is so much fresh green peppercorn grown in Bali that we wanted to use it in our desserts as well as our savoury dishes. We found the chocolate was strong enough to contain the heat of the peppercorn, while still allowing its rich chocolatey aroma to come through. Accented with lime leaf, the combination is a perfect balance of heat, richness and acidity.

*Elements of this recipe should be prepared 1 day in advance.

PORTION: Serves 10 **DIFFICULTY LEVEL:** 🍴🍴🍴

INGREDIENTS

Jelly
100 ml water
2 tbsp sugar
½ tsp fresh green peppercorns
1 leaf gelatine, pre-soaked
1⅔ tbsp lime juice

Lady Fingers
3 eggs, separated
50 g sugar
50 g plain flour, sifted
5½ tsp cocoa powder, sifted

Mousse
200 ml milk
28 kaffir lime leaves
2½ egg yolks
50 g sugar
120 g dark chocolate, chopped
2 leaves gelatine, pre-soaked
225 ml cream (retain 10 tsp of the whipped cream for garnish)

Reduction
200 ml red wine
200 g grapes, pitted
½ tsp mixed peppercorns (black, white, andaliman and Java comet tail)
¼ tsp orange zest, finely grated
6 cm cassia bark
2 tbsp liquid glucose

Chocolate Glaze
125 ml cream
45 kaffir lime leaves, chopped
125 g sugar
250 g dark chocolate, chopped
1 tsp lime zest, finely grated
4 tbsp cocoa powder
125 g ice cubes

METHOD

Make the jelly in advance. Bring the water, sugar and peppercorns to the boil, then remove from the heat, cover and infuse for 20 minutes. Add the gelatine and stir until it has dissolved. When it's cool, add the lime juice. Pour the liquid into the smaller moulds, making sure that each mould gets roughly the same number of green peppercorns. Freeze.

To make the lady fingers, preheat the oven to 160°C. Beat the egg whites and sugar together until stiff peaks form (like a meringue). Beat the egg yolks to break them, then add them to the meringue and fold to combine. Fold in the cocoa and flour. Using a spatula, spread the mixture thinly (about 5 mm) on a baking tray lined with a non-stick mat or baking paper. Bake for approximately 8 minutes. Cool, then cut into 10 x 6 cm circles using a cutter or one of the large moulds.

To prepare the larger moulds, place them on a baking tray and line the inside walls of each mould with plastic mica that has been cut to size. Place a circle of lady finger at the bottom of each mould. Remove the frozen jellies from the moulds, returning the de-moulded ones to the freezer until you have finished this task. Working quickly so the jellies don't melt, place a frozen jelly in the centre of each mould, using melted chocolate to glue the jelly to the lady finger. Freeze until firm.

For the mousse, bring the milk to the boil and add the lime leaves. Remove from the heat, cover and allow to infuse for 20 minutes. Make a sabayon by beating the egg yolks and sugar together in a stainless-steel bowl over a pan of simmering water until thick and smooth (5–10 minutes). Bring the milk back to the boil, then remove from the heat. Allow it to cool for a few minutes, until it reaches 80°C. Strain and then add the milk to the sabayon and mix well. Add the chocolate, stirring until it has completely melted. Add the gelatine and stir to dissolve. Allow to cool to room temperature.

Meanwhile, whip the cream to soft peaks. When the chocolate mixture has cooled (the mixture shouldn't set), add the whipped cream and fold it in. Don't overmix or the lightness of the whipped cream will be lost, but make sure the whipped cream has been fully incorporated into the chocolate with no lumps of whipped cream remaining. Place the mixture in a measuring jug and pour it into the moulds so it fills the space around the peppercorn jelly and covers it by at least 1 cm. Freeze until firm.

To make the pepper reduction, place all the ingredients in a saucepan over medium heat and bring to the boil, reducing the mixture so that the sauce is suitable for drizzling on a plate. Allow it to cool.

To make the chocolate glaze, bring the cream to the boil and add the chopped lime leaves. Remove from the heat, cover and allow to infuse for 1 hour. Strain. Stir the sugar in a pan over medium heat until it melts and caramelises (approximately 5 minutes). Bring the cream back to the boil, then deglaze the caramel with the hot cream by adding it gradually, and stirring continuously (the cream and caramel should be the same temperature). Remove from the heat. Add the chocolate, lime zest and cocoa and stir until the chocolate has melted and the mixture is combined. Add the ice cubes one at a time, stirring continuously (this will ensure the glaze is nice and shiny). Use immediately.

Crisps
2 limes, zest only, peeled
3½ tbsp sugar
120 g plain white rice, cooked
2½ tbsp glutinous rice flour
1 tbsp cocoa powder

Peaches
2½ yellow peaches, quartered, skin on
2½ tbsp icing sugar

Condiments and Garnishes
10 fresh herb tips
10 tsp whipped cream (reserved from the whipped cream for the Lime Mousse)

Special Equipment
10 moulds 2 cm wide x 3 cm tall*
10 moulds 6 cm wide x 4½ cm tall
plastic mica (a sturdy plastic sheet that can be cut into strips for lining the moulds)

* It's OK to use different-sized moulds, but one should always be half the size of the other, and be able to fit inside it. If commercial moulds are not available, they can be made using PVC pipe.

Remove the mousses from the freezer and put them on a wire rack with a pan underneath. Using a large spoon, pour a spoonful of glaze over each mousse so they are covered in a thin layer of chocolate glaze. Refrigerate. Please note: once the mousses are glazed, they should be stored in the refrigerator. Do not freeze them.

To make the crisps, preheat the oven to 110°C. Cover the peeled zest with water and bring it to the boil. Strain and rinse thoroughly. Repeat this 3 times. Blend all the ingredients until smooth. Strain. Place spoonfuls of batter on a non-stick mat or baking paper and spread each one with a spoon into circles that are 1 mm thick and 7–8 cm in diameter. Bake for 15 minutes. Flip and bake for 60 minutes or until crispy. Cool to room temperature and store in an airtight container.

To roast the peaches, preheat the oven to 200°C. Place them on a baking tray and sprinkle with icing sugar. Roast the peaches for 10–15 minutes or until golden-brown, but still holding their shape. Remove from the oven and allow them to cool. When cool, remove the skins from the peaches.

Remove the mousses from the refrigerator and make sure the jelly in each mousse has defrosted by gently inserting a toothpick into it. If the jelly is still frozen, let the mousses sit at room temperature until they have defrosted, then serve immediately, or the mousse may break apart.

When you are ready to serve, decorate each plate with the pepper reduction. Place a chocolate mousse on each plate. Top the mousse with a scoop, or quenelle, of whipped cream, pieces of cocoa-lime crisp and a fresh herb sprig. Put a slice of roasted peach on each plate. Serve immediately.

TIP

For information on making a caramel, see Techniques (page 140).

ceviche of langoustine on the half shell with andaliman pepper and caviar

ABOUT THE RECIPE: It took us a while to discover andaliman pepper. I first came across this pepper when I cooked with it in Malaysia. My suppliers in Indonesia were stumped when I asked why andaliman pepper wasn't available here, and they promised to look into the matter. Sure enough, a sample of the product arrived on Mozaic's doorstep several months later, marking the start of a whole new string of recipes, including this dish. This recipe came about when we were playing around with the subtle flavour and texture of langoustines, prepared raw or slightly cured. Langoustines have such a rich and creamy taste, requiring only the most subtle seasoning and some acidity. Adding andaliman pepper allowed us to introduce a gentle, peppery, but yet pronounced lemony flavour to the ceviche. Because andaliman pepper is only mildly hot, it doesn't overpower the overall flavours of this dish.

PORTION: Serves 4 as an appetiser **DIFFICULTY LEVEL:**

INGREDIENTS

Langoustines

6 langoustines, heads removed, tails split lengthwise in half with shells intact
100 ml lemon juice
100 ml olive oil
1 tsp orange zest, finely grated
1 tsp lemon zest, finely grated
½ tsp lime zest, finely grated
1 pinch salt

Vodka Cream (reserve 12 tsp for garnish)

½ tbsp lemon zest, julienned
65 g crème fraîche
1 tsp vodka (or more if you prefer)
juice from 1 lemon wedge
salt and white pepper, to taste

Andaliman Pepper Lavosh (makes 15 servings)

100 g plain flour (or more if required)
2 tbsp sugar
2 tbsp butter, unsalted, melted
1 tsp salt
½ egg
3 tbsp milk
1 egg (for egg wash)
1 tbsp water
ground andaliman pepper, to taste
sea salt, to taste

Balsamic Reduction

85 ml good quality balsamic vinegar
50 g liquid glucose
75 g dark muscat-style grapes
10 lemon verbena leaves

Condiments and Garnishes

1 tbsp shallots, chopped
1 tbsp chives, chopped
2 fresh laksa leaves, finely sliced
sea salt, to taste
andaliman peppers, dry roasted, to taste
12 tsp Vodka Cream (recipe above)
6 tsp caviar
12 portions of Andaliman Pepper Lavosh (recipe above)
½ punnet micro-coriander leaves

METHOD

To prepare the langoustines, mix all the ingredients except the langoustines together to form a marinade and immerse the langoustines in it Refrigerate for 2–3 hours. If you are preparing this dish well ahead of time, take the langoustines from the marinade after the prescribed amount of time, cover with cling film and refrigerate until you are ready to use them.

To make the vodka cream, cover the julienned zest with water and bring it to the boil. Strain and rinse thoroughly. Repeat this twice. Combine all the ingredients and season to taste with salt and pepper. Add more vodka if you wish. Refrigerate for a minimum of 1 hour to allow the cream to set.

To make the lavosh, put the flour, salt, sugar, butter, egg and milk in a small dough mixer and mix until you have a smooth dough. Using a pasta roller, roll out the dough until it's as thin as possible without breaking. Cut the dough into small right-angled triangles of approximately 1½ cm wide x 4 cm tall. Combine the whole egg and water to form an egg wash and brush the triangles with it. Sprinkle them with andaliman pepper and sea salt. Bake at 160°C for approximately 20 minutes or until golden-brown. Allow to cool to room temperature and store them in an airtight container.

For the reduction, place all the ingredients in a saucepan and simmer until the grapes break open. Strain the mixture through a sieve, pushing down on it to extract all the juices. Reduce the sauce to a consistency that is suitable for drizzling on a plate. Strain again with a fine sieve. Season to taste with salt and a little more balsamic vinegar if needed. Set aside.

To assemble, take the langoustines from the refrigerator and season them with the shallots, chives, laksa leaves, sea salt and pepper. Decorate each plate using the reduction. Place 3 langoustine halves on each plate. Top each half with a scoop, or quenelle, of vodka cream, followed by some caviar. Garnish with 3 pieces of pepper lavosh and a sprinkle of micro-coriander leaves. Serve immediately.

TIP

Andaliman pepper is very versatile. Use it for curing, seasoning and smoking any seafood or meat, such as salmon or duck breast; the taste is amazing. You could substitute it with a mixture of Szechuan pepper and lemon zest, though it wouldn't be exactly the same.

JACKFRUIT

Artocarpus heterophyllus L. (*Moraceae*)
Balinese/Indonesian/Malay: *nangka*

FOOD CHARACTER

Jackfruit has a distinctive structure with meat-like fibres and large nut-like oval seeds. Young and mature, ripe jackfruit have very different qualities. The young jackfruit has a pale-yellow colour and mild vegetable taste, something like artichoke. It absorbs flavours well, making it excellent in heavily spiced stews, where it can easily be mistaken for meat. Ripe jackfruit, on the other hand, has deep golden-yellow flesh and a heavy perfume that evokes a blend of pineapple, gardenia and banana.

PHYSICALS

Jackfruit is the largest edible fruit on earth. It can grow up to 1 metre long and weigh up to 50 kg. Indonesia has over 30 varieties of jackfruit, 20 of which are found in Java. Jackfruit bears fruit and flowers all year, but the mature tree (over five years old) may produce only 15–18 fruits annually.

LOCAL USE

Young jackfruit is used as a vegetable (*jukut nangka*) and cooked with basa gede spices (see page 105). Ripe jackfruit is eaten raw or used in coconut milk desserts such as *cendol*. The seeds are dried and ground to provide flour, which is used in food processing. The famous Indonesian stew, *gudeg*, from Central Java features jackfruit. Jackfruit wood is prized for furniture and musical instruments.

NOTES FROM CHEF SALANS

Ripe jackfruit is a bit like durian in that it has a very strong and exotic flavour. Luckily, it doesn't smell as bad as durian, so it's a bit easier to tolerate. Like mango and papaya, Asians consume this both ripe as a fruit and unripe as a vegetable. I'm not aware of any Western fruit that is consumed both ripe and unripe, except possibly certain tomatoes. It's this aspect of the jackfruit that I really like and have tried to help you discover in the following recipes.

Selecting the ingredient: As a vegetable, young, unripe jackfruit should be like most vegetables: nice and firm without bruises or dents. In Asia, it's often sold already peeled. Ripe jackfruit can be purchased whole in its shell, or peeled. For ripe jackfruit, choose one that is deep yellow in colour; I find that lighter coloured jackfruit is less flavoursome. Overripe fruits will taste too strong or may even be fermented. When the fruit is growing, the spikes of the skin are bunched closely together and are approximately 0.5–1.5 cm in height. Once the fruit ripens, the spikes spread and flatten.

How to prepare it: When preparing young jackfruit, wear gloves and protect your cutting board with parchment paper or plastic, because the fruit exudes a sticky sap that is difficult to wash off (remove the sap on your knife by rubbing it with a cloth and a little cooking oil). Blanch the young jackfruit to remove the sap. It should be cooked al dente (don't overcook it as it will fall apart) before being used for other preparations. When dealing with ripe jackfruit, remove the outer and inner filaments to expose the fruit. Then, cut open the fruit and remove the seed and the skin surrounding it. Although I haven't used the seeds of the ripe or unripe jackfruit in the recipes here, they are great either boiled or roasted like chestnuts.

Substitutes: Jackfruit can also be purchased frozen, dried or canned either in brine (usually unripe) or in syrup (ripe).

OPPOSITE Young, unripe jackfruit (left) is used as a vegetable, while mature, ripe jackfruit (right) is eaten as a fruit.
THIS PAGE Ripe jackfruit (left) and young jackfruit (right) cut open to reveal their different compositions.

young jackfruit and cèpe mushroom soup with cèpe satays

ABOUT THE RECIPE: This is another of Mozaic's early classics. When I first tasted jackfruit in its unripe vegetable form, it instantly reminded me of an artichoke. When I started discovering Balinese flavours, I think I subconsciously tried to associate new flavours with those my palate was already familiar with, so for me artichoke it was and artichoke it still is. I have used the original Balinese method of cooking jackfruit in this recipe – as a stew spiced with basa gede (see page 105) – but I also integrated a Western flavour, the cèpe (or porcini) mushroom and, more importantly, a Western texture: creaminess. This soup is another example of a dish where the classic flavours of Balinese cuisine have been retained. While the dish appears to be entirely Western, it offers the diner a pleasantly familiar yet completely surprising experience.

PORTION: Serves 4 to 5 as an appetiser **DIFFICULTY LEVEL:** 🍴🍴🍴

INGREDIENTS

Mushroom Oil
75 g cèpe (porcini) mushrooms
100 ml salad oil

Jackfruit Stew
125 g young unripe jackfruit, peeled and cut into 2 cm slices
2 tsp Basa Gede (see page 107)
250 ml chicken stock, see Techniques (page 140)
½ stalk lemongrass, crushed
1 salam leaf
salt and white pepper, to taste

Soup
1 quantity Jackfruit Stew (recipe above)
1 quantity Cèpe Oil (recipe above)
100 ml cream

Satays
100 g cèpe mushrooms, cut into 1½ x 1½ cm cubes
salt and pepper, to taste
2 tbsp salad oil

Garnish
5 fresh herb sprigs of your choice

METHOD

To prepare the mushroom oil, gently simmer the 2 ingredients in a saucepan over low heat for 60 minutes, stirring occasionally to make sure the mushrooms don't stick. Cool to room temperature.

To make the jackfruit stew, place the jackfruit slices in a saucepan, cover with water and bring to the boil. Simmer until the jackfruit is half-cooked; the fruit should be firmer than al dente. Strain.

Bring the jackfruit and the remaining ingredients to the boil and simmer them until the jackfruit is soft enough to be puréed. Remove the salam leaf and lemongrass stalk, and blend until smooth.

To make the soup, blend the jackfruit stew, gradually adding the mushrooms and their oil. Strain the mixture and pour it into a saucepan. Bring the soup to the boil and add the cream. Season to taste with salt and pepper.

To prepare the mushroom satays, thread the cubed mushrooms onto 5 pre-soaked wooden skewers. Season them with salt and pepper, then grill or sear the skewers in the oil.

To serve, pour some soup into the preheated bowls and top each one with a cèpe skewer. Garnish with a fresh herb sprig and serve immediately.

TIPS

Cèpe oil is readily available nowadays, but unfortunately it's often artificially flavoured. Therefore, we make our own cèpe oil at Mozaic.

This soup also works well as a sauce or broth for meat, seafood or vegetables.

rack of lamb with balsamic reduction, cardamom gelée and jackfruit salad

ABOUT THE RECIPE: I love ripe jackfruit. It has a unique, almost intoxicating flavour. This recipe is an intense and bold way of using this fruit. I like the sophisticated balance between the intriguing flavour of jackfruit and the acidity of the balsamic reduction. They work very well together to form a perfect match. If paired cleverly, a ripe and intense-tasting fruit can enhance a savoury dish and make it come alive. Keep this principle in mind and you can successfully incorporate most types of fruit into your repertoire of dishes and create some complex and delicious flavour profiles.

PORTION: Serves 6 as an appetiser or 3 as a main course **DIFFICULTY LEVEL:**

INGREDIENTS

Reduction
10 cardamom pods
50 ml Martini Bianco
50 ml Martini Rosso
200 ml balsamic vinegar

Jelly
2 cardamom pods, seeds only
water, as needed
50 ml UHT milk
1 tsp sugar
1 ½ tsp milk powder
½ tsp plain konnyaku jelly powder (Nutrijell or any other quality brand)

Dukkah
50 g hazelnuts
4 tsp white sesame seeds
4 tsp black sesame seeds
3 tbsp coriander seeds
1 pinch salt
2 pinches sumac
2 tbsp honey

Eggplant Caviar
500 g eggplants
2 tbsp extra virgin olive oil
salt and white pepper, to taste
100 ml extra virgin olive oil
1 tbsp garlic, roasted
1 tbsp chives, sliced

Lamb
2 racks of lamb
salt and pepper, to taste
2 tbsp salad oil

Cardamom-Verbena Demi-Glaçe
5 cardamom pods, cracked
500 ml beef demi-glaçe, see Techniques (page 140)
1 sprig lemon verbena
1 bulb ripe jackfruit
salt and pepper, to taste

Jackfruit Salad
6 bulbs ripe jackfruit, diced
2 tsp shallots, chopped
2 tsp walnuts, toasted and chopped
1 tsp flat leaf parsley, chopped
1 tsp fresh ginger juice
1 tbsp walnut oil
1 tsp lemon juice
salt and pepper, to taste

Garnish
6 fresh herb sprigs of your choice

METHOD

To make the reduction, bruise the cardamom pods, then dry roast them in a pan over low heat. Stir for 2–3 minutes until the cardamom smells slightly toasty, but not burnt. Remove from the heat and add the remaining ingredients. Return to the heat and simmer, reducing the liquid by approximately three-quarters, or until it's of a syrupy consistency. Set aside.

To make the jelly, dry roast the cardamom seeds over low heat until they are fragrant. Add enough water to cover the seeds, and simmer for a few minutes. Blend or grind the mixture into a rough purée. Combine it with the milk, sugar and milk powder in a saucepan and bring to the boil. Add the konnyaku jelly powder and whisk continuously, so the mixture doesn't burn. Boil for 1 minute, then pour into a container; the depth of the liquid should be approximately 1 ½ cm. Cool to room temperature and cut into cubes measuring 1 ½ x 1 ½ cm. Set aside.

For the dukkah, roast the hazelnuts in a 180–200°C oven until dark golden-brown. Remove from the oven, and roll the nuts around in a kitchen towel while hot and apply pressure to remove their skins. Crush the hazelnuts roughly with a mortar and pestle. Combine the nuts with the black and white sesame seeds, salt, sumac and honey, and mix thoroughly. Spread the mixture over a non-stick mat and bake at 130°C for 30 minutes. Remove from the oven and let the dukkah brittle cool to room temperature. Break the brittle by hand into a rough crumble and store it in an airtight container.

To prepare the eggplant caviar, preheat the oven to 200°C with a roasting tray inside. Cut the eggplants in half, leaving their peduncles on. Season with the 2 tbsp of olive oil, salt and pepper. Place on the preheated roasting tray and roast until the eggplants are very soft. Allow to cool to room temperature. Scoop out the flesh, including the brown, roasted parts. Place the flesh in a strainer and allow it to drain in the refrigerator for a minimum of 2 hours. Combine the refrigerated eggplant pulp with 100 ml of extra virgin olive oil and the garlic, and blend in a food processor. Season to taste with salt and pepper. Set aside.

To cook the lamb, preheat the oven to 200°C with a roasting pan set with a rack. Season the lamb with salt and pepper. Heat the oil in a sauté pan over medium to high heat and sear the lamb until it's brown all over. Place the lamb on the rack in the oven. Close the oven door and turn the heat off immediately. Allow the meat to cook in the residual heat for a minimum of 1 hour. Don't open the oven door during this time. The meat should be rare when it comes out of the oven.

To make the demi-glaçe, dry roast the cardamom pods over low heat until they are fragrant. Add the demi-glaçe and bring it to the boil. Add the lemon verbena and jackfruit. Cover with a lid, set aside and allow it to infuse for 10 minutes. Adjust the seasoning and set aside.

For the jackfruit salad, mix all the ingredients well, adjusting the seasoning as needed.

To assemble, cut each rack of lamb into 3 pieces. Trim any excess fat and remove the bones, so that only 1 bone remains per portion. Season with salt and pepper, and reheat in the oven (160–180°C) until it's done to your liking. Also reheat the demi-glaçe and eggplant caviar. When the eggplant is hot, mix in the chives.

Decorate each pre-warmed plate with a drizzle of the reduction and a piece of cardamom from the reduction. Arrange a spoonful of jackfruit salad, a quenelle of eggplant caviar, 2 cubes of jelly and a few spoonfuls of dukkah crumble on each plate. Place the lamb on top of the jackfruit salad, and drizzle the demi-glaçe over it. Garnish with a fresh herb sprig and serve immediately.

TIPS

I particularly like the slow-cooking technique for lamb used in this recipe. This method allows the meat to cook and rest at the same time. You get delicious meat that is juicy, tender, evenly red and perfectly cooked. Even though the meat comes out of the oven rare, it can be reheated to any level of doneness. You will find that well-done lamb cooked this way far surpasses that cooked over direct heat.

You can adapt my easy technique of transforming dukkah into a crumble, using a spice mixture of your own. It adds a great kick to any dish.

crispy duck and young jackfruit civet with ripe jackfruit relish and wild cress sauce

ABOUT THE RECIPE: This is an early Mozaic recipe and it features both the unripened and ripened flavours of jackfruit. I was inspired by a wonderful artichoke and cèpe *civet* (a French technique for cooking game in a red wine stew) we used to make at David Bouley's. The rich texture of the *civet* combined with the hearty flavour of the duck is sensational. The ripe jackfruit gives a sweet and sour hint to the dish and lifts it to the realm of the extraordinary. I have always avoided serving duck breast because of its high fat content, so in this recipe, I have developed a technique where the fat is rendered, leaving a nice crisp skin that encases the moist flesh beneath.

PORTION: Serves 6 as an appetiser or 3 as a main course   **DIFFICULTY LEVEL:**

INGREDIENTS

Civet
240 g young jackfruit, peeled, cut into 2 cm slices
60 ml salad oil
2 tbsp plain flour
80 g cèpe (porcini) mushrooms
10 g butter
1 tbsp shallots, finely chopped
½ tsp thyme leaves
50 g garlic, roasted, see Techniques (page 140)
100 ml good red wine
100 ml beef demi-glaçe, see Techniques (page 140)
salt and pepper, to taste
2 tbsp flat leaf parsley, chopped

Cress Sauce
1 large white onion, skin on
200 g Balinese wild cress (use regular cress if unavailable)
2 tbsp salad oil
salt and pepper, to taste

Duck
2 duck breasts, skin on, 250 g each
salt and pepper, to taste

Relish
80 g ripe jackfruit, cut into thin strips
2 tbsp walnut oil
½ lemon, juice only
5 walnut halves, roasted and chopped
1 tbsp fresh ginger juice
2 tsp flat leaf parsley, chopped
salt and pepper, to taste

Garnish
6 fresh herb sprigs of your choice

METHOD

To prepare the civet, boil the young jackfruit until it's half-cooked. Refrigerate until cold, then cut into bite-size segments. Season with salt, pepper and flour. Heat half the oil in a frypan over medium to high heat, and sear the jackfruit until it's golden-brown. Remove the jackfruit from the pan and add the remaining oil. Once hot, add the mushrooms and sear them until they are golden-brown. Remove the mushrooms, turn the heat down to medium and add the butter to the pan. Add the shallots and thyme and cook for 1 minute. Add half the garlic and squash it with the back of a spoon. Give the mixture a stir, then pour in the red wine. Allow the wine to reduce by three-quarters. Add the jackfruit, mushrooms, remaining garlic and demi-glaçe. Simmer and reduce slightly before adding salt and pepper to taste, then stir in the parsley. Set aside for a minimum of 1 hour before use; better yet, make this the day before and refrigerate it for 12–24 hours, then reheat before use. If the jackfruit is not tender by the time the stew is too thick, add some water to the stew to thin it and continue cooking.

To make the cress sauce, wrap the onion in aluminium foil and roast it in a 180°C oven for 1–1½ hours until the onion is very soft. Remove it from the oven and allow it to cool down a little. Peel the onion and blend it into a smooth purée. Strain and set aside. Heat the oil in a hot wok and quickly stir-fry the cress. Remove the cress and plunge it immediately into a basin of ice water to stop the cooking process and ensure that the cress retains its vivid green colour. Drain the cress and remove the excess water, reserving the water for the sauce. Place the cress in a blender and add just enough of the water so the cress can be blended into a smooth purée. Strain. Pour the purée into a saucepan and add 1–2 tbsp of puréed onion. Adjust the consistency with a little of the reserved water, so the puree is suitable for plate decorating. Season to taste with salt and pepper.

Meanwhile, prepare the duck breasts. Clean the meat of sinew, but be sure to leave the fat intact as it will protect the meat during the cooking process. Use a sharp knife to score the fat side of the duck breast in a crisscross pattern; be sure to cut deep into the fat but not through to the meat. Season the duck with salt and pepper on the meat side only. Heat a pan over medium heat and, using no oil, place the duck breast in the pan, fat side down. Allow to sear until 1 or 2 tbsp of fat are rendered. Pour off the fat and continue cooking the duck, rendering more fat in the process. It's important to regulate the heat to make sure the duck doesn't burn. As more fat is released, you will need to reduce the heat. Cook until all the fat has been rendered, but make sure the duck is not more than half-cooked (depending on the thickness of the breast, the temperature of the pan and the type of pan used, whether cast iron or stainless steel; this should take approximately 5 minutes). Flip the duck, turn off the heat, take the pan off the stove and allow the duck to cook gently in the residual heat of the pan for approximately 10 minutes. Remove the meat from the pan, and rest it for a minimum of 5 minutes before serving.

To prepare the relish, season the ripe jackfruit with the remaining ingredients and mix thoroughly.

To assemble, slice the duck breasts and reheat them in a hot oven. Pour the cress sauce into the bowls. Spoon the jackfruit civet into the centre. Remove the duck from the oven and arrange the slices on top of the civet. Heap the relish on top of the duck, garnish with a fresh herb sprig and serve immediately.

TIP

Making the civet between one and several days in advance will enhance the flavours of the stew and further improve the texture of the jackfruit.

STARFRUIT AND BELIMBING WULUH

STARFRUIT
Averrhoa carambola (*Oxalidaceae*)
Balinese/Indonesian: *belimbing*
Also known as: carambola, star apple

BELIMBING WULUH
Averrhoa bilimbi (*Oxalidaceae*)
Indonesian: *belimbing sayur*
Balinese: *belimbing wuluh* (*buluh*)
Also known as: bilimbi, cucumber tree, pickle fruit

FOOD CHARACTER

The starfruit, so named because when cross-sectioned it looks like a five-pointed star, is a tart to mildly sweet, astringent, and very juicy fruit with a flavour that recalls a combination of orange, papaya, pineapple and grapefruit. Its texture is tender and fleshy. Its relative, the belimbing wuluh, is crisp and very sour with bright green, jelly-like flesh and a similar starfruit flavour, though much more acidic.

PHYSICALS

The starfruit is native to Southeast Asia, where it grows on a relatively short bushy tree with deciduous leaves that are sensitive to light. At perfect ripeness, the fruit is yellow with a tinge of green; as it ripens further the ridges turn brown. The skin is thin and waxy; the entire fruit, along with its tiny seeds, is edible. Starfruit is generally 6–15 cm long. The much smaller belimbing wuluh is 4–10 cm long, with barely discernible star ridges. When ripe, belimbing wuluh becomes yellow-green. Both fruits are widely cultivated in Southeast Asia.

OPPOSITE The sweet and tangy starfruit and very tart belimbing wuluh can both be used as fruit or vegetables.
THIS PAGE Starfruit (left) and belimbing wuluh (right), sliced and ready for use.

LOCAL USE

Starfruit is consumed raw or as a juice. The young leaves of *belimbing besi* (a sour variety of starfruit) are sometimes featured in the Balinese dish called *lawar*. Belimbing wuluh is used for tartness in seasoning. In Java, it's used as a vegetable (*sayur* means "vegetable" in Indonesian) in soups and stews, where its sourness works well with the richness of coconut milk.

NOTES FROM CHEF SALANS

Though starfruit and belimbing wuluh are very different, they pair up well together. The very sour belimbing wuluh beautifully complements the starfruit, which is sweet but lacks acidity. The starfruit is another interesting example of a fruit used as a vegetable when young and unripe. Both fruits can also be used on their own, as you will see in the following recipes.

Selecting the ingredient: The starfruit used in these recipes should be chosen as ripe as possible so that they are sweet. They should be yellow with the edges just starting to turn brown. It's often better to buy the fruit slightly under-ripe and let it ripen at home under your watchful eye as it tends to quickly over-ripen overnight. Belimbing wuluh should also be selected as ripe as possible and without bruises or holes. When young, they are small, very firm and dark green. When ripe, belimbing wuluh are larger (approximately 6 cm long and 2 cm wide), pale green to yellow and, though firm, easily crushed with your fingers.

How to prepare it: Starfruit, as a ripe and sweet fruit, can be served raw or as a juice. It can also be sliced and used in cooking. Starfruit should be cleaned and the protruding extremities should be cut off before use. Belimbing wuluh should simply be cleaned and the ends trimmed.

Substitutes: There is no substitute for starfruit and belimbing wuluh other than another fruit that is sour when young and unripe, and sweet when ripe, such as mangoes or pineapple. Belimbing wuluh could be substituted with a young, unripe, very green and sour starfruit.

pan-seared foie gras with sweet and sour belimbing wuluh broth

ABOUT THE RECIPE: Thinking back on the story behind this recipe makes me laugh to this day. An American friend living in Bali visited Mozaic one day, and told me that he had eaten foie gras with belimbing wuluh in a restaurant in New York City. What jolting news – here I was in the capital of belimbing wuluh and not doing anything with them, while someone thousands of miles away from any belimbing wuluh tree was using them. Spurred on to do something about it, I confined myself to the kitchen until I managed to put belimbing wuluh on the menu in many different ways. I discovered that I can tone down the acidity of any sour ingredient with slow cooking in a sugar syrup. In this simple dish, I unite the acidity of belimbing wuluh and the sweetness of its cooking syrup with the crispiness of seared foie gras to bring about a delectable and unexpected result.

*Elements of this recipe should be prepared 1 day in advance.

PORTION: Serves 6 as an appetiser or 3 as a main course

DIFFICULTY LEVEL:

INGREDIENTS

Belimbing Wuluh Confit
400 ml water
200 g sugar
16 cm piece cassia bark
2 tbsp coriander seeds
½ vanilla bean, halved lengthwise
7 star anise, whole
½ tsp orange zest, finely grated
½ tsp lemon zest, finely grated
1 sprig mint
200 g belimbing wuluh, cut into 2 cm pieces

Starfruit Chips
½ green, unripe starfruit, cut into 1 mm slices
100 g sugar
100 g (not ml) water

Belimbing Wuluh for the Foie Gras
30 confied belimbing wuluh (recipe above)
100 ml syrup (from Belimbing Wuluh Confit)
100 ml belimbing wuluh juice
salt and pepper, to taste

Foie Gras
6 slices foie gras, grade A, 60 g each (or 3 x 120 g)
salt and pepper, to taste
6 tbsp shallots, sliced
1 tsp thyme leaves
sea salt, to taste

Broth
100 ml chicken stock, see Techniques (page 140)
1 tbsp chives, chopped

Garnish
6 fresh herb sprigs of your choice

METHOD

Make the belimbing wuluh confit in advance. Place all the ingredients except the belimbing wuluh in a saucepan and simmer for 15 minutes. Add the belimbing wuluh. Bring to the boil and simmer for 1 minute. With the belimbing wuluh slices still in the syrup, set aside to cool to room temperature. Refrigerate for a minimum of 12 hours.

To make the starfruit chips, bring the sugar and water to the boil, stirring to dissolve the sugar. Set aside to cool to room temperature. Preheat the oven to 60–80°C. Place the starfruit slices in the cool sugar syrup, stirring gently to ensure the slices are evenly coated. Remove from the syrup and drain on paper towels, then arrange the slices on a non-stick mat or baking paper. Dry them for 2–3 hours in the oven until crispy. Store in an airtight container.

To prepare the belimbing wuluh for the foie gras, combine all the ingredients in a saucepan and bring to the boil. Remove from the heat and set aside.

Season the foie gras slices with salt and pepper. Sauté the foie gras in a pan over medium to high heat until they are golden-brown on both sides. Reduce the heat and cook the slices until the centre of the foie gras is warm to the touch. Reduce the heat further and, with the foie gras still in the pan, add the shallots and thyme. Fry them gently for a minute until the shallots are translucent. Remove the foie gras and shallots from the pan, season with sea salt and set aside. Deglaze the frying pan with the chicken stock to form a broth. Add the broth to the saucepan containing the confied belimbing wuluh, syrup and juice, and bring to the boil. Remove from the heat, then add the chives and adjust the seasoning. Use immediately so the chives don't turn brown.

To assemble, take some confied belimbing wuluh from the broth and place it in the centre of the pre-warmed bowls. Put a slice of foie gras on top and spoon some broth around it. Top with a starfruit chip and a fresh herb sprig.

TIPS

Belimbing wuluh is not easily available. You might want to try Asian speciality markets, or substitute them with very green, unripe starfruit.

For information on simple syrups and setting very low oven temperatures, see Techniques (page 140).

carpaccio of starfruit, belimbing wuluh, strawberries and mint

ABOUT THE RECIPE: This recipe is a great way to pair starfruit and belimbing wuluh, which are usually not served together. Belimbing wuluh is almost unbearable to eat because of its high acidity, but when combined with the sweetness of ripe starfruit, which lacks natural acidity, you get a starfruit carpaccio that is made in heaven. The starfruit sorbet is similarly improved by the addition of belimbing wuluh juice. Not only does it increase the acidity of the sorbet, it also adds a wonderful aroma. The accompanying mint salad is a sweet interpretation of the spicy Balinese *sambal matah*. In my version, strawberries are mixed with tangy mint leaves and finished with shallots and a pinch of salt. I thought of adding shrimp paste (*terasi*), but I think some taste buds may be too challenged!

*Elements of this recipe should be prepared 1 day in advance.

PORTION: Serves 10 **DIFFICULTY LEVEL:**

INGREDIENTS

Belimbing Wuluh Confit
400 ml water
200 g sugar
16 cm piece cassia bark
2 tbsp coriander seeds
½ vanilla bean, halved lengthwise
7 star anise, whole
½ tsp orange zest, finely grated
½ tsp lemon zest, finely grated
1 sprig mint
200 g belimbing wuluh, cut into 2 cm pieces

Starfruit Chips
½ green, unripe starfruit, cut into 1 mm slices
100 g sugar
100 g (not ml) water

Sorbet
300 ml starfruit juice
100 ml liquid glucose
2 tsp sugar
1 leaf gelatine, pre-soaked
2 tbsp belimbing wuluh juice
2 tsp fresh passion fruit juice

Starfruit Carpaccio
3 ripe starfruit, cut into 2 mm slices
10 tsp syrup (from Belimbing Wuluh Confit)
1 tbsp lemon juice
50 confied belimbing wuluh (recipe above)

Mint Salad
20 strawberries, sliced
10 tbsp mint leaves
10 tsp syrup (from Belimbing Wuluh Confit)
10 tsp shallots, finely sliced
1 pinch salt
ground black pepper, to taste

METHOD

Make the confied belimbing wuluh in advance. Place all the ingredients except the belimbing wuluh in a saucepan and simmer for 15 minutes. Add the belimbing wuluh. Bring to the boil and simmer for 1 minute. With the belimbing wuluh slices still in the syrup, set aside to cool to room temperature. Refrigerate for a minimum of 12 hours.

To make the starfruit chips, bring the sugar and water to the boil, stirring to dissolve the sugar. Set aside to cool to room temperature. Preheat the oven to 60–80°C. Place the starfruit slices in the syrup, stirring gently to ensure they are coated. Remove from the syrup and drain on paper towels, then arrange the slices on a non-stick mat or baking paper. Dry them for 2–3 hours in the oven until crispy. Store in an airtight container.

For the sorbet, bring 50 ml of the starfruit juice, the glucose and the sugar to the boil. Stir until the sugar dissolves. Remove from the heat, add the gelatine and stir to dissolve. Add the remaining ingredients and stir. Refrigerate until chilled, then churn the mixture in an ice cream machine until it hardens. Transfer the sorbet to a plastic container and freeze.

To prepare the carpaccio, divide the starfruit slices among the plates, overlapping them lengthwise to form a line on each plate (or in a circle if you are using round plates). Mix the syrup with the lemon juice, and drizzle it over the carpaccio. Place 5 confied belimbing wuluh on each plate.

For the mint salad, mix all the ingredients and season to taste with the syrup, salt and pepper.

To serve, place a scoop, or quenelle, of sorbet on top of each carpaccio. Top with some mint salad and 2 starfruit chips. Serve immediately.

TIPS

Use only ripe starfruit that have turned almost yellow. If unavailable, any ripe, acidic fruit in season will work equally well.

For information on simple syrups, setting very low oven temperatures and how to make sorbet if you don't have an ice cream machine, see Techniques (page 140).

ROOT SPICES: GALANGAL, GINGER AND TURMERIC

Galangal, ginger and turmeric are important anchors in the Indonesian spice palette. Greater galangal, *Alpinia galanga* [L.] *Willd*. (*Zingiberaceae*), is called *laos* in Indonesian, *isèn* in Balinese and *khaa* in Thai. It's also known as blue ginger and China root. Fresh ginger, *Zingiber officinale* (*Zingiberaceae*), often called ginger root, is known as *jahe* in Indonesian and Balinese. Turmeric, *Curcuma longa Linn*. (*Zingiberaceae*), is called *kunyit* in Indonesian and Balinese; it's sometimes called Indian saffron, although it has no relation to saffron.

FOOD CHARACTER

Raw galangal has an earthy aroma with traces of citrus, pine, cedar, camphor and soap (it contains saponins), and a certain amount of heat. Ginger brings a pleasant warmth to both sweet and savoury dishes. Very young ginger is sometimes pickled, and the young green shoots can be eaten raw. Turmeric's intense yellow hue makes it an important culinary dye. Its aroma is earthy and slightly acrid; its flavour is slightly warm, rather bitter and can be penetrating.

PHYSICALS

Galangal is a tall plant with blade-like leaves and white lily-like flowers. Its rhizome has distinctive orange-brown skin marked by rings and a crisp whitish flesh. The ginger plant is a tall, creeping plant that can reach up to 3 metres high, with blade-like leaves and small yellow-green flowers. The ginger rhizome is thick and bulbous, with a pale brown skin and yellow flesh. In contrast, the turmeric plant is relatively short, with long-stemmed leaves and small yellow flowers. The turmeric rhizome has a light-brown ringed skin and orange flesh.

LOCAL USE

Greater galangal is used in the more complex spice mixtures of Indonesia, as well as the tongue-searing *tom yum* soups of Thailand. Ginger is a basic ingredient found in all Indonesian spice mixtures. Sliced ginger root is often infused in coffee or tea as a flavouring ingredient and to bring warmth. Ginger infusion and ginger candy are especially effective in preventing motion sickness. Turmeric is used in Indonesian spice mixtures, especially those used to cook eggs or fish. In Bali, *nasi kuning* (yellow rice), which is flavoured with turmeric, is served on the first day of the 210-day calendar.

NOTES FROM CHEF SALANS

Galangal, ginger and turmeric are well known and should be easy to find – if not fresh, they can sometimes be found frozen. Two other root spices used in Indonesian cuisine – *kencur* (aromatic ginger) and *temu kunci* (finger root) – are also pictured opposite.

Selecting the ingredient: Root spices should be plump and firm, with no bruises or insect holes. If they are very fresh, they may be covered in soil; clean them off to check their quality. When cracked open, they should have pronounced colours. Turmeric should be bright orange; ginger, golden-yellow; galangal, pink; and aromatic ginger and finger root, white. All should be moist, and water should seep out when they are cracked.

How to prepare it: Root spices should be cleaned and peeled before being used. They can be bruised and tossed into dishes, or they can be sliced, chopped or further ground in a mortar, food processor or blender. Fresh root spices can be stored up to a month or more in the refrigerator if they are wiped dry, wrapped in paper towels and placed in a ziplock bag.

Substitutes: Powdered root spices aren't recommended for these recipes as the taste would be different and probably not as pleasant.

OPPOSITE A tray of root spices with their characteristic colours: pink galangal, yellow ginger, yellow and blue aromatic ginger, orange turmeric and white finger root.
THIS PAGE *Left to right*: ginger, turmeric and galangal, ready for use in preparations.

langoustines in a tea of bumbu kuning

ABOUT THE RECIPE: Although much of Balinese cuisine is based on the traditional basa gede spice mix, a variety of other spice mixes are used, like those for fish, shellfish, and red and white meat. This recipe introduces a special blend known as *bumbu kuning*, which literally means "yellow spice mix". It may be named after its colour (in line with the simplicity of Balinese cuisine), but its flavour is sensational and it demonstrates the potential of Balinese cuisine featuring on the world stage. In this recipe, we have modernised this traditional spice mix by making an infusion with it. It was done in the spirit of a French bouillabaise, by infusing the spices in a shellfish stock laced with a little Pernod for an evocative twist.

PORTION: Serves 10 as an appetiser **DIFFICULTY LEVEL:**

INGREDIENTS

Langoustine Stock (yields 1.2 litres)
20 large langoustines
2 litres water
salt and white pepper, to taste

Consommé
1.2 litres Langoustine Stock (recipe above)
100 g galangal, coarsely sliced
50 g ginger, coarsely sliced
6 lemongrass stalks, coarsely sliced
5 lime leaves, torn
5 salam leaves (or bay leaves), torn
4 cloves garlic, coarsely sliced

METHOD

To make the langoustine stock, clean the langoustine heads and shells by rinsing them under cold water. Roast them at 200–220°C until the shells turn bright orange and a little brown at the edges. Then place the roasted shells in a saucepan with the water and salt, and gently simmer for 45 minutes. Remove from the heat and allow it to cool to room temperature. Strain. Reduce the stock until you get a strong but pleasant langoustine flavour. Season to taste with salt and pepper.

For the consommé, combine all the ingredients in a teapot (or saucepan) and gently simmer for 30 minutes. Set aside. Add the Pernod to taste and season to taste with salt and pepper.

4 shallots, coarsely sliced
2 cm turmeric, coarsely sliced
2 bird's eye chillies, deseeded and coarsely sliced
1 tomato, sliced
1 tbsp anise-based alcohol, such as Pernod or Ricard

Condiments and Garnishes

1–2 carrots, cut into strips and cooked al dente
100 g white shimeji mushrooms
10 green asparagus, sliced and cooked al dente
10 fennel (or other edible) flowers
10 lemon basil (or other aromatic) leaves

Next, prepare the tea cups. Arrange 2 langoustine tails, a carrot strip, some mushrooms, slices of asparagus, a fennel flower and a lemon basil leaf in each cup. Serve immediately, or keep at room temperature (for a short time only) before use. If you are preparing the dish ahead of time and prefer to refrigerate it for freshness, remember to take the cups out of the refrigerator approximately 30 minutes before serving to bring them to room temperature.

To serve, pour the boiling hot broth from the teapot or saucepan directly into the tea cups to poach the langoustine tails gently. Serve immediately.

TIPS

You can apply the principle and technique of this recipe to any traditional recipe or spice mix from Bali or other regions, and it will work just as well.

Making a proper consommé requires a lot of painstaking work, so I have re-worked the langoustine stock in this recipe to make it easier

seasonal exotic fruits marinated in spiced passion fruit broth

ABOUT THE RECIPE: This is an awesome dish that boasts very full flavours. Those with a milder palate might find this dessert too overbearing and in-your-face but, in my opinion, it's a great way to experience Indonesian root spices. Here is a perfect example of what two creative minds – my former pastry chef François Seurin and I – can do when put together in the same kitchen. A mix of root spices, used in traditional Balinese cooking, infused in syrup and emulsified with sour passion fruit pulp makes an amazing and powerful treat for the senses. Pair this foamy broth with traditional crème brûlée and some crisps, and you get an unforgettable dessert with both creamy and crunchy textures that will balance out the intensity of the spices.

PORTION: Serves 10 **DIFFICULTY LEVEL:**

INGREDIENTS

Sorbet
230 ml water
65 ml honey
100 ml liquid glucose
1 leaf gelatine, pre-soaked
165 ml plain unsweetened yoghurt
1½ tbsp lemon juice

Candied Orange Peel
2 oranges, skin only
100 g sugar
100 g (not ml) water

Crème Brûlée
200 ml milk
½ vanilla bean
200 ml cream
4 egg yolks
25 g fine sugar
50 g coconut palm sugar

Milk Crisps
120 g white rice, steamed
2½ tbsp glutinous rice flour
3½ tbsp milk powder
3½ tbsp fine sugar
1 tsp lime zest, finely grated

Broth
375 ml water
100 g sugar
30 g ginger, grated
20 g galangal, grated
15 g turmeric, grated
¼ orange, zest only, peeled
¼ lime, zest only, peeled
½ vanilla bean, cut lengthwise
175 g passion fruit pulp, without seeds
¼ tsp soya lecithin (or more if needed)

Fruit Salad
(cleaned and cut to even-sized shapes)
100 g mango
100 g pink guava
100 g starfruit
100 g kiwi fruit
100 g palm fruit
100 g lychee
100 g banana
100 g rosewater apple

Garnishes
10 fresh herb sprigs of your choice
30 strips candied orange peel (recipe above)

Special Equipment
ice cream machine

METHOD

To make the sorbet, place the water, glucose and honey in a saucepan and bring to the boil. Remove it from the heat and add the gelatine, stirring until it has dissolved. Allow it to cool to room temperature. Add the lemon juice and yoghurt, and whisk until smooth. Refrigerate until chilled, then churn the sorbet in an ice cream machine until it hardens. Transfer the sorbet to a plastic container and freeze.

To prepare the candied orange peel, cut the skin (ie, zest and white pith) off the oranges with a sharp knife and set aside the peeled fruit for later use. Cover the skins with water and bring to the boil. Strain and rinse thoroughly. Repeat this process 4 more times. Place the blanched skin, sugar and water in a saucepan over very low heat, and gently simmer until a thick syrup forms. Taste the skin; it should be tender and sweet. If not, add a little water and continue cooking. Remove from the heat and allow it to cool to room temperature. Remove the skins from the syrup and and cut them into ½ cm wide strips. Set aside.

To prepare the crème brûlée, preheat the oven to 110°C and place a roasting pan of water in the oven (as a bain marie). Split the vanilla bean and scrape out the seeds. In a saucepan, put the milk, vanilla seeds and bean, and the cream, then bring the mixture to the boil before removing it from the heat. Whisk the egg yolks and sugar in a mixing bowl until the eggs start to froth and turn pale. Pour half of the warm milk and cream mixture (make sure it's not more than 85°C) onto the egg yolks. Mix thoroughly, then pour this mixture back into the saucepan with the rest of the milk and cream mixture. Strain the mixture and pour it into a square mould. The depth of the crème brûlée in the mould should be 2 cm. Place the mould in the bain marie (be careful not to get any water in the mould) and bake it for approximately 20 minutes. The mixture should have the texture of a custard and not be too liquid or runny. Once done, remove it from the oven and allow it to cool to room temperature. Refrigerate.

For the milk crisps, preheat the oven to 110°C. Blend all the ingredients together in a processor or blender until the mixture is smooth and has a batter-like consistency. Strain. Place spoonfuls of batter on a non-stick mat or baking paper and spread each one with a spoon into circles that are 1 mm thick and 7–8 cm in diameter. Bake for 15 minutes. Flip them and bake for 1 hour, or until crispy. Allow the crisps to cool to room temperature, then store them in an airtight container.

Next, make the broth. Place the water, sugar, root spices, zest and vanilla bean and seeds (split and seeds extracted) in a saucepan and bring to the boil. Remove the saucepan from the heat, cover with a lid and allow it to infuse for 30 minutes. Strain the mixture through a fine sieve, then mix in the passion fruit pulp. Blend the mixture until it's smooth. Add the soya lecithin and blend the liquid with a hand blender to develop a strong foam. Add more soya lecithin if needed.

To assemble, divide the fruit neatly among the bowls, keeping the centres of the bowls empty. Refrigerate. Sprinkle a layer of palm sugar on top of the crème brûlée and, using a blowtorch, make a nice firm crust of caramel (adding more layers of sugar as needed to achieve this). Cut the crème brûlée into 10 squares. Place a square in the centre of each bowl. Emulsify the passion fruit broth with a hand blender until froth forms on top. Top each crème brûlée with a scoop, or quenelle, of sorbet, some passion fruit broth and the foam. Garnish with the candied orange peel, a milk crisp and a fresh herb sprig. Serve immediately.

TIPS

Try this recipe with different root spices, substituting with lemongrass or any fresh Asian herb. The same goes for the fruit. Just use any fruit in season that is sweet and ripe. This is really the secret to great cooking – you can never go wrong when using the finest ingredients.

For information on simple syrups and how to make sorbet if you don't have an ice cream machine, see Techniques (page 140).

wagyu carpaccio in rendang oil with cèpe mushrooms and parmesan emulsion

ABOUT THE RECIPE: *Rendang* is a spicy and ambrosial beef dish frequently served in Indonesian restaurants. Chunks of beef are simmered in coconut milk and a *rendang* spice mix for hours until the coconut milk splits and the resulting oil fries the meat. As beef *rendang* is a staple dish that is eaten day in and day out in Indonesia, I wanted to introduce its flavours on my menu, but in an adapted form. We started experimenting with flavoured oils and infusing all kinds of Indonesian spice mixes in them before we finally perfected the formula – a *rendang* oil that is almost sweet tasting due to the coconut (almost, because it's still quite spicy). The idea was to serve this flavoured oil as simply as possible, so that all of its delicate aromas could be savoured. We paired the *rendang* oil with a premium beef carpaccio. Married with meaty cèpe mushrooms and a light foam of full-bodied Parmesan, the dish is well balanced and utterly addictive – just the way a fine carpaccio should be.

*Elements of this recipe should be prepared 1 day in advance.

PORTION: Serves 6 as an appetiser **DIFFICULTY LEVEL:**

INGREDIENTS

Rendang Oil

3 coconuts, grated
80 g aren palm sugar, crumbled

For the paste:

8 Lombok chillies (or red chillies), deseeded
2 hot Balinese chillies, deseeded
50 g ginger, unpeeled
90 g turmeric, unpeeled
45 g lesser galangal, unpeeled
2½ tbsp coriander seeds
2½ tsp fennel seeds
1½ tsp caraway seeds
1 tsp cumin seeds
½ tsp white peppercorns
½ tsp black peppercorns
180 g shallots, peeled
70 g garlic, peeled
4 candlenuts
1 tsp shrimp paste, grilled

1 litre salad oil

To be used whole:

3 cloves
10 cm cassia bark
450 ml fresh coconut milk
4 lemongrass stalks, bruised
60 g galangal, peeled and bruised
4 turmeric leaves, bruised
4 kaffir lime leaves, bruised
3 salam leaves, bruised
1 tbsp salt
200 g beef trimmings, cut into small pieces

Parmesan Foam

100 g good quality Parmesan cheese, grated
100 ml water
salt and white pepper, to taste
¼ tsp soya lecithin powder (or more if needed)

Beef Carpaccio

240 g sirloin of wagyu beef, grade 9+, cleaned
3 tbsp Rendang Oil (recipe above)
sea salt and black pepper, to taste
3 tbsp shallots, chopped
3 tbsp chives, chopped
2 tbsp Parmesan cheese, grated

Cèpe Mushrooms

210 g cèpe (porcini) mushrooms, cut into 2 cm chunks
1 tbsp salad oil
salt and white pepper, to taste
sea salt, to taste

Garnish

6 sprigs chervil

METHOD

Make the rendang oil in advance. Roast the grated coconut in an 120°C oven for approximately 1 hour until it turns golden-brown and dries out. Stir it regularly to ensure even roasting. Approximately 5 minutes before removing the coconut from the oven, add the palm sugar. Mix well, and allow it to cool to room temperature. Set aside.

Meanwhile, clean both the red and Balinese chillies and boil them in water until soft. Set aside. Grill the ginger, turmeric and lesser galangal until their skins loosen and start to fall off. Remove them from the grill and peel them. Dry roast all the seeds and peppercorns in a pan until they are fragrant. Using a mortar and pestle, grind all the ingredients (marked "for the paste") to form a smooth paste. Alternatively, blend them in a food processor. Sauté the paste in salad oil until it's fragrant.

Place the paste, roasted coconut and the remaining ingredients (marked "to be used whole") in a large saucepan, and gently cook them for 2 hours. Stir the mixture regularly so it doesn't burn. Remove the saucepan from the heat and allow it to cool to room temperature. Refrigerate for a minimum of 12 hours, then strain to get the oil. Refrigerate. To maximise the shelf life of the rendang oil, store it in an airtight container and avoid exposure to light.

To make the Parmesan foam, combine the Parmesan cheese and water in a saucepan and bring to the boil, stirring occasionally with a spoon. Remove from the heat, cover with a lid and allow to infuse for 15 minutes. Mix well, ensuring there is no cheese stuck to the bottom of the saucepan. Strain the liquid, pressing down on the cheese to extract as much flavour as possible. Season with salt, if needed, and pepper (the taste of the pepper should be obvious, so don't be afraid of adding extra pepper to achieve this). Add the soya lecithin and blend the liquid with a hand blender to develop a strong foam. Add more soya lecithin if needed.

For the beef carpaccio, first freeze the beef. Slice the frozen beef as thinly as possible with a meat slicer or sharp knife. Divide the slices among the plates, arranging them in a circle around each plate without overlapping. Cover with cling film and refrigerate.

To prepare the mushrooms, heat the oil in a pan and sear them until they are golden-brown. Season to taste with salt and pepper, then drain them on paper towels. Season with sea salt. Use immediately.

To assemble, take the plates of carpaccio from the refrigerator and remove the cling film. Drizzle the rendang oil over the meat then season it with sea salt and black pepper. Sprinkle the shallots and chives over the meat. Place some grated Parmesan in the centre of each carpaccio, making sure the circle of cheese is not larger than 5–6 cm. Top the grated cheese with a large spoonful of Parmesan foam, covering it completely. The foam should be nice, tall and light enough so it doesn't spread or run on the plate. Finally, place the mushrooms around the carpaccio and garnish with the chervil.

TIP

Flavoured oils keep for a long time, so go ahead and make extra for future use. These oils can be used in dressings or simply for cooking (sautéing, barbecuing, etc). Keep flavoured oils in an airtight container away from heat and light, or in a refrigerator.

BASA GEDE

FOOD CHARACTER

Basa gede is a Balinese term meaning "grand spice mixture" and contains a variety of roots, spices, and fresh and fermented aromatics. It's usually pungent and very hot, though it can be adjusted to taste.

LOCAL USE

In addition to its ubiquitous role in Balinese home cooking, basa gede also features in the great festive dishes of Bali, including spit-roasted whole pig (*babi guling*), smoked duck (*bebek betutu*) and meat salads called *lawar*. Before dawn, on the morning of ceremonial occasions, Balinese men from the community will get together to slaughter and cook the sacrificial animals and prepare the basa gede from scratch. Not all parts of the animals end up as either *babi guling* or *bebek betutu*; much of the meat is made into satay, both for offerings and to feed the hundreds of guests invited to these ceremonies. The cheaper cuts are simmered in stews spiced with basa gede and mixed with blanched leaves or vegetables, *sambal* (a spicy condiment), fresh coconut and often blood, to create *lawar*.

NOTES FROM CHEF SALANS

Basa gede is the base of all Balinese cuisine. Mastering it is a mandatory step in understanding all Balinese dishes, and for that reason it deserves an entire chapter in this book. Though there are different versions of basa gede, I have kept the version in this cookbook as simple as possible so that it's easier for home cooks to recreate.

Selecting the ingredients: As with root spices, the ingredients for basa gede should be as fresh as possible (for further information on root spices, see page 97).

How to prepare: Using a mortar and pestle is time-consuming and takes practice, so I suggest using either a food processor or, better yet, a meat grinder. The flavour is not exactly the same as grinding the paste by hand, but the time and effort saved is worth taking this shortcut, especially when preparing large amounts. Basa gede can be made in advance and stored for a long time in the refrigerator or freezer.

Substitutes: There is no substitute for basa gede. However, it's possible to recreate the recipes in this chapter with an entirely different mix of spices – either exotic or traditional.

OPPOSITE Basa gede ingredients, *clockwise from top*: galangal, lemongrass, hot chillies, aromatic ginger, candlenuts, ginger, salam leaves, salt, white peppercorns, red chillies and turmeric, with shallots, garlic and shrimp paste in the centre.
THIS PAGE TOP Basa gede ingredients being ground.
THIS PAGE BOTTOM The ubiquitous *babi guling*, Balinese spit-roasted whole suckling pig from the famous Warung Babi Guling, Ibu Oka in Ubud.

crispy pork belly marinated in basa gede, curried onion stew and parmesan foam

ABOUT THE RECIPE: Basa gede is so integral to Balinese cuisine that I can't recall the first time I tasted it; I have probably eaten very few Balinese meals where basa gede didn't feature as an ingredient. The traditional Balinese roasted pork, *babi guling*, is one of my favourite dishes featuring this spice mix. In this delicious rendition, we use basa gede and pork belly, but marry them in a completely different and more modern way. I believe that Ubud, the home of Mozaic, has the best *babi guling* in Bali and arguably the world. It's one of the true wonders of Balinese cuisine, and a mystical experience for me each time I get to eat it. If there is one thing you shouldn't leave Bali without trying, it's the *babi guling* from Ubud, with sweet tender flesh and crisp crackling.

*This recipe requires a long cooking time.

PORTION: Serves 10 as an appetiser or 5 as a main course

DIFFICULTY LEVEL:

INGREDIENTS

Basa Gede

300 g shallots
100 g garlic cloves, whole
75 g galangal, roughly chopped
75 g ginger, roughly chopped
60 g fresh turmeric, roughly chopped
60 g lesser galangal, roughly chopped
3 candlenuts
200 g Lombok chillies (or red chillies), deseeded
8 bird's eye chillies, deseeded
1 tsp shrimp paste
2 salam leaves
2 lemongrass stalks
1 tsp white peppercorns, whole
1 tsp salt
100 ml salad oil

Pork Belly

1 kg pork belly
200 g Basa Gede (recipe above)
salt, to taste
sea salt, as needed for baking

Onion Stew

15 g butter
8 fresh curry leaves
1 tsp Madras curry powder
250 g onion, peeled and sliced
1 tbsp raisins
salt and white pepper, to taste

Parmesan Foam

200 g good quality Parmesan cheese, grated
200 ml water
salt and white pepper, to taste
1/4 tsp soya lecithin powder (or more if needed)

Pork Sauce

1 tbsp pork fat, from the cooked pork
10 fresh curry leaves
200 ml beef demi-glaçe, see Techniques (page 140)
1 tsp fresh ginger juice
2 tbsp Basa Gede Oil (see page 109)
salt and black pepper, to taste

Garnish

10 fresh herb sprigs of your choice

Special Equipment

combi-steam oven

METHOD

Make the basa gede in advance. Grind all the ingredients with mortar and pestle by hand (or use a food processor or, preferably, a meat grinder). Heat the oil in a large pan and cook the mixture over low heat for 1 hour, stirring every few minutes to ensure the mixture doesn't stick or burn. Remove from the heat and allow to cool to room temperature. Refrigerate until cold.

To cook the pork, season it well with salt, then spread the basa gede onto the meat side (not skin side). Wrap it in cling film and refrigerate for a minimum of 2 hours. Remove the cling film and place the pork belly skin side down on an oven rack. Place the rack in a combi-steam oven with a roasting pan underneath to catch any dripping juices or fat (if you don't have a combi-steam oven, try placing a pan of water in a traditional oven; see Tips below). Set the oven to steam-roast at 105°C, and cook the pork belly for 8 hours. Remove the pork from the oven and reserve 2 tbsp of the pork fat from the roasting pan. Place a heavy tray on top of the pork to put pressure on it, then refrigerate until cold. Once cold, remove and discard the basa gede spices. Cut the pork and its skin into 10 equal portions. If there is still excess fat in the meat, open the layers of meat up if necessary to remove it. Use the trimmings from portioning the pork to fill any gaps in the meat. Refrigerate for a minimum of 4 hours to allow the meat to set.

To make the onion stew, place a saucepan over medium heat and sauté the curry leaves in the butter. Stir in the Madras curry powder, then the sliced onions and a big pinch of salt. Mix well. Cover the saucepan with a lid and cook over low heat until the onions have softened and are half-submerged in liquid (this is due to the onions releasing water). This should take approximately 15–20 minutes. Remove the aluminium foil, add the raisins and stir well. Continue to simmer uncovered until the liquid has evaporated and the onions are tender and melt in your mouth. If the onions aren't yet tender, add a little water or chicken stock and continue to cook them until they reach the desired tenderness.

To make the Parmesan foam, combine the Parmesan cheese and water in a saucepan and bring to the boil, stirring occasionally with a spoon. Remove from the heat, cover with a lid and allow to infuse for 15 minutes. Mix well, ensuring there is no cheese stuck to the bottom of the saucepan. Strain the liquid, pressing down on the cheese to extract as much flavour as possible. Season with salt, if needed, and pepper (the taste of the pepper should be obvious, so don't be afraid of adding extra pepper to achieve this). Add the soya lecithin and blend the liquid with a hand blender to develop a strong foam. Add more soya lecithin if needed.

To prepare the pork sauce, put the pork fat in a small saucepan over medium heat. When the fat is lightly smoking, add the curry leaves and fry until they are crispy. Add the demi-glaçe, ginger juice and basa gede oil. Bring to the boil. Season with salt and pepper and set aside.

To assemble, preheat the oven to 200°C. Spread a thin layer of sea salt over a roasting pan or baking tray, and place the pork portions skin-side down on the salt. Bake for 12–15 minutes or until the pork is warm inside and the skin is nice and crispy. Separate the crispy skin from the meat; if necessary, remove any excess sea salt that may have stuck to the skin.

Preheat the bowls and place 2 spoonfuls of onion stew in each bowl. Top with a piece of pork belly without the skin. Spoon the pork sauce over the meat, ensuring each portion gets 1 curry leaf. Place the skin on top of the pork.

Emulsify the Parmesan foam and spread it evenly around the pork (no liquid from the emulsion should be added, only the foam). Top with a fresh herb sprig and serve immediately.

TIPS

Pork belly is full of fat, and in this day and age of healthy eating, many people are wary of cooking it. This cooking method reduces the fat content in the meat by rendering the fat without drying the meat out, and then crisping up the skin.

We use a combi-steam oven to cook the pork belly as it gives a lovely, moist result. If you don't have a combi-steam oven, you can pour a couple of litres of water in a roasting pan and place it in a hot oven. Once the water is hot, place the pork belly on a rack suspended over the roasting pan. Although not quite as effective as a combi-steam oven, this steamy environment will ensure better results than traditional oven roasting.

basa gede-confied salmon fillet with gingered apple purée, salad and caviar

ABOUT THE RECIPE: There are countless ways of using basa gede, but one of the more unusual is as a flavouring for an infused oil. In this recipe, basa gede is cooked in a much larger quantity of oil and then refrigerated for 12 hours. The mixture is then strained and only the oil is used. This flavoured oil can be used for cooking, as a dip for breads, whisked into dressings or in myriad other ways. In this dish, fish is submerged in basa gede oil and then gently cooked. The French technique of "confit" is well known for the extremely moist and tender results it produces, but it also allows you to discreetly infuse flavours into the fish using flavoured oils. I encourage you to try making your own infused oils and cooking fish this way. It's truly amazing, and the flavours are limited only by your imagination.

*Elements of this recipe should be prepared 1 day in advance.

PORTION: Serves 4 as an appetiser or 2 as a main course

DIFFICULTY LEVEL:

INGREDIENTS

Basa Gede Oil
300 g shallots
100 g garlic cloves, whole
75 g galangal, roughly chopped
75 g ginger, roughly chopped
60 g fresh turmeric
60 g lesser galangal, roughly chopped
3 candlenuts
200 g Lombok chillies (or red chillies), deseeded
8 bird's eye chillies, deseeded
1 tsp shrimp paste
2 salam leaves
2 lemongrass stalks
1 tsp white peppercorns, whole
1 tsp salt
1 litre salad oil

Apple Purée
25 g butter, unsalted
2 tsp ginger, chopped
2 small apples, peeled, cored and diced
salt, to taste

Apple Jelly
60 ml water
5 stalks lemongrass, bruised
1 gala apple, peeled, cored and sliced
1 tbsp lemon juice
2 tbsp frozen granny smith apple purée (Boiron or any other quality brand)
2 tsp plain konnyaku jelly powder (Nutrijell or any other quality brand)
1 drop green food colouring
1 tsp extra virgin olive oil
salt and pepper, to taste

Salmon
320 g salmon fillet, 4 x 80 g or 2 x 160 g portions
salt and pepper, to taste
250 ml Basa Gede Oil (recipe above)
sea salt, to taste

Apple Salad
1 gala apple, julienned
1 tbsp walnut oil
1 tsp walnuts, roasted and crushed
½ tsp flat leaf parsley, chopped
½ tsp lemon juice
½ tsp fresh ginger juice
salt and white pepper, to taste

Condiments and Garnishes
4 tsp crème fraîche
4 tsp caviar
12 mini capers, pan fried or deep fried
2 walnuts, roasted and broken into pieces
4 fresh herb sprigs of your choice

METHOD

Make the basa gede oil in advance. Grind all the ingredients with a mortar and pestle (or a food processor or, preferably, a meat grincer). Heat the oil in a large pan and cook the mixture over low heat for 1 hour, stirring every few minutes to ensure the mixture doesn't stick or burn. Remove from the heat and allow to cool to room temperature. Refrigerate for a minimum of 12 hours, then strain to get the oil. To maximise the shelf life of the basa gede oil, store it in an airtight container in the refrigerator and avoid exposure to light.

To make the apple purée, melt the butter in a saucepan and cook the ginger slowly over low heat. When the ginger is translucent, add the diced apple. Put a lid on the pan and simmer until the apple is cooked. Blend in a processor and strain. Adjust the seasoning, then set aside.

To prepare the apple jelly, place the water and bruised lemongrass in a saucepan and bring it to the boil, then cover, set aside, and allow it to infuse for 20 minutes. Blend the apple with the lemon juice in a food processor until smooth. Add the strained lemongrass water, puréed apple, Nutrigell powder and food colouring and bring it to the boil over medium heat. Boil for 30 seconds, whisking continuously so that the mixture doesn't burn. Pour into a container so the liquid reaches a depth of 1½ cm. Cool to room temperature and cut into 1½ x 1½ cm cubes. Season with olive oil, and salt and pepper to taste. Set aside.

At least 1 hour before serving, prepare the salmon. Preheat the oven to 50°C. Season the fillets and place them in an ovenproof dish in a single layer with some space between them so the fillets don't stick together. Add enough basa gede oil to cover the fish by at least 1 cm. Place the tray in the oven and cook for 30–40 minutes. The fish should look undercooked, but break apart easily when pressed with a fork. Remove the tray from the oven and take the fish out of the oil, draining it on paper towels. Season with sea salt.

Prepare the apple salad by mixing all the ingredients together.

Spoon some of the warm apple purée onto the centre of each plate. Place 2 pieces of apple jelly, 2 pieces of walnut and 2 or 3 capers around the plate.

Reheat the confied fish in a 140°C oven for no more than 1 minute (so that it retains its beautiful colour and texture). Place a portion of fish in the centre of the purée. Top each portion with the salad, a quenelle of crème fraîche, a tsp of caviar and a fresh herb sprig. Serve immediately.

TIPS

At Mozaic, we use a lot of ginger juice and having a fresh supply on hand is essential, but the problem is the juice oxidizes and, instead of remaining acidic, it becomes sour. So, rather than juicing the ginger (as well as our other root spices), my staff grate it. The grated ginger keeps for 3 or 4 days in the refrigerator and whenever we need juice, we simply squeeze the grated pulp for a fresh supply.

For information on setting very low oven temperatures, see Techniques (page 140).

TAMARIND

Tamarindus indica L. (*Caesalpiniaceae/Leguminosae*)
Indonesian/Malay: *asam* (*asem*), *asam Jawa*
Balinese: *lunak*
Also known as: date of India

FOOD CHARACTER

Tamarind is both slightly sweet and highly acidic at the same time, with a fruity, sour taste (*asam* means "sour" in Indonesian) that combines well with the heat of chillies and other spices. It's an important ingredient in chutneys, and is perhaps best known in the West for the tartness it lends to Worcestershire sauce. In Mexico, it's bottled as a fizzy soda.

PHYSICALS

The tamarind tree, native to tropical Africa and long naturalised throughout the tropical world, grows to a height of some 20 metres or more and has fine, feathery leaves. The fruits are bean-like pods with a sticky pulp enclosing large black seeds. Tamarind has many medicinal uses, particularly in aiding digestion and reducing flatulence; the juice can also be used as an antiseptic.

LOCAL USE

In the heat of the afternoon, a popular snack in Bali is the spicy fruit salad called *rujak*, in which fruit and cooling vegetables, such as cucumber and jicama (*bangkuang*) are served with a rich, dark sauce of tamarind, palm sugar, shrimp paste and chillies.

NOTES FROM CHEF SALANS

Tamarind is great in both savoury and sweet preparations, though it always needs some sweetness to balance out its acidity. In the following recipes, we focus on traditional *rujak* sauce and demonstrate how it can be used in more complex ways than with the simple (yet excellent) Indonesian fruit salad.
Selecting the ingredient: Tamarind is usually sold as a paste, in a tube or a block. It can also be purchased fresh in its shell, but it's difficult to judge the quality, and preparing it in its fresh form is time-consuming. Tamarind varies from very light brown to dark brown. I prefer medium-brown tamarind; too dark and it will be too ripe and more sweet than sour, although all levels of ripeness seem to have their specific applications.
How to prepare it: To remove the seeds and fibres, mix the paste with hot water to form a mixture thin enough to strain. The liquid is then used in preparations, either alone or mixed with spices, sugar and other ingredients.
Substitutes: There is no substitute for tamarind, but it should be fairly easy to find in an Asian grocery store. There is also a candied version of tamarind, which I haven't tried but could perhaps be used for the recipes here, although the amount of sugar in the recipe would need to be reduced.

OPPOSITE The aromatic and astringent tamarind fruit on the tree.
THIS PAGE Tamarind in the hull, with the seeds removed, and after soaking and straining.

rock lobster with rujak sauce, barley risotto and girolle mushrooms

ABOUT THE RECIPE: I like the way *rujak* sauce is used in this recipe. When I first tasted *rujak* sauce, I found it a little hard to swallow (most Westerners will tell you that *rujak* is an acquired taste). The sweet and sour sauce is usually served with fruits as part of a dessert or snack, and yet it contains strong-tasting fermented shrimp paste as well as a lot of chilli. To make it more acceptable to the general palate, I modified the sauce. I removed some of the chilli to make things a little more subtle, and instead of using shrimp paste, I added concentrated lobster stock to lend a delicate, savoury shellfish taste to the sauce. When this *rujak* sauce is paired with a creamy "risotto" made with barley and an intense yet sweetly flavoured mushroom like girolle, the dish turns out to be unconventional yet delightful.

PORTION: Serves 6 as an appetiser or 3 as a main course **DIFFICULTY LEVEL:**

INGREDIENTS

Lobsters and Stock
6 rock lobsters, 350 g each, cleaned
(or 3 lobsters, 650–750 g each)
approx 1 litre water
salt and white pepper, to taste
unsalted butter, as needed

Rujak Sauce
1 pinch salt
¼ bird's eye chilli
2 tsp tamarind pulp
3 tbsp aren palm sugar
50 ml Lobster Stock (recipe above)

Mushrooms
5 g butter, unsalted
1 tsp salad oil
50 g girolle mushrooms
salt and pepper, to taste
1 tbsp shallots, chopped
1 tsp thyme leaves
3 tbsp chicken stock, see Techniques (page 140)

Risotto
100 g barley, uncooked
15 g butter, unsalted
1 tbsp shallots, finely chopped
1 pinch thyme leaves
100 ml Lobster Stock (recipe above)
50 ml cream
2 tbsp Parmesan cheese, grated
1 tbsp chives, chopped

Spinach
35 g butter, unsalted
6 cloves garlic, roasted, see Techniques (page 140)
3 tbsp shallots, chopped
250 g spinach leaves, stems removed
salt and white pepper, to taste

Garnish
6 fresh herb sprigs of your choice

METHOD

To prepare the stock, remove the lobster heads and set aside the tails for later use. Chop the heads into smaller pieces. Rinse under running water, drain well and roast in a 200°C oven until the shells turn bright orange and a little brown at the edges. Remove the roasted heads from the oven and place them in a saucepan containing a pinch of salt and enough water to cover the lobster trimmings by approximately 2 cm. Simmer gently for 1 hour regularly skimming off any impurities that rise to the surface. Remove the stock from the heat and allow it to rest for 30 minutes. Strain. The recipe should yield approximately 400 ml of stock. Pour half of it (200 ml) into a saucepan and reduce it about 100 ml for a more intense flavour. Season with salt and pepper, and reserve for cooking the risotto. Reduce the remaining 200 ml of stock by boiling it over high heat until the stock attains a thick, almost syrupy consistency (approximately 50 ml). Set it aside for the rujak sauce.

To make the rujak sauce, grind the salt and chilli with a mortar and pestle. In a bowl, combine the tamarind pulp, palm sugar and thick lobster stock syrup and massage it by hand until it has dissolved. Strain. Pour it gradually into the mortar and mix well. Adjust the consistency with hot water to obtain a smooth and creamy sauce. Set aside.

For the mushrooms, heat the butter and oil in a sauté pan over medium to high heat. When it begins to bubble, add the mushrooms and allow them to brown lightly. Season with salt and pepper to taste. Add the shallots and thyme, turning the heat to low so the shallots don't burn. Toss lightly and let the shallots cook gently. Add the chicken stock then set aside.

If you are using small lobsters, the tails should be cooked whole (otherwise, cut large lobster tails in half). Any method of cooking can be used; the tails can be simmered in court bouillon, steamed, grilled, roasted or cooked in any manner to your liking. At Mozaic, we poach the lobster tails in a pot of melted butter for 20 minutes (use a thermometer to check that the butter temperature is no higher than 60°C). Then we remove the tails from the butter, slice them and sprinkle them with sea salt.

To make the barley risotto, boil the barley in a saucepan of water (alternatively, cook it in a steamer) until the barley is half-cooked and still quite firm. Strain and rinse with cold water. Melt the butter in a pan, and add the shallots and thyme, cooking them until the shallots are translucent. Add the precooked barley and mix well. Divide the 100 ml of lobster stock in half and add one half to the pan, stirring continuously until the stock has been absorbed by the barley. Then gradually add the other half of the stock, stirring continuously until the barley is al dente (tender yet slighty resistant). Add the mushrooms, then the cream and simmer the risotto until it is creamy. Use immediately.

To sauté the spinach, lightly brown the butter in a pan over medium heat. Add the shallots and garlic, then remove the pan from the heat and add the spinach leaves. Toss quickly, allowing the spinach to wilt. Season to taste with salt and pepper.

Decorate the plates using the rujak sauce. Shape a small mound of spinach on each plate and arrange the slices of lobster on the spinach. Place a scoop, or quenelle, of barley risotto on the plate, and sprinkle some Parmesan cheese and chives over the risotto. Garnish with a fresh herb sprig and serve immediately.

TIP

A rock lobster is a spiny lobster with no claws. The French call it *langouste*, while the Australians call it crayfish. Although this recipe uses rock lobsters, you can substitute it with most other types of lobsters. Because traditional lobster stock is not easy to make, I've created a simplified version for this recipe.

langoustines wrapped in mushrooms with basa gede-rujak dressing

ABOUT THE RECIPE: The natural sourness of tamarind makes it a great substitute for vinegar or lemon juice. Not only does it lighten flavours with its acidity, it also adds a hint of exoticism to dishes with its subtle flavour. But tamarind is not the only star ingredient in the following recipe. One comes across so many beautiful tropical fruits in Bali, it's a shame not to use them in as many ways as possible. What better way than to incorporate them in a savoury dish to bring out their savoury qualities and textures, which are all too often overlooked? Featuring exotic fruit, tamarind and basa gede, this dish is a perfect balance of sweet, savoury and sour.

PORTION: Serves 4 as an appetiser **DIFFICULTY LEVEL:** 🍴🍴🍴

INGREDIENTS

Spiced Syrup (makes 10 x 4 servings)
250 ml water
60 g sugar
1 tbsp coriander seeds
4 cm cassia bark
1 star anise, whole
1 clove
1 strip orange zest, peeled
1 strip lime zest, peeled
½ sprig mint

Langoustines
6 langoustines
18 slices cèpe mushroom, finely sliced lengthwise
salt and white pepper, to taste
1 tbsp salad oil
15 g butter, unsalted
1 tbsp shallots, chopped
2 pinches thyme leaves

Langoustine Stock
20 langoustine, heads and trimmings only
650 ml water
tiny pinch salt
salt and white pepper, to taste

Fennel Purée
1 bulb fennel, leaves removed

Rujak Sauce
1 pinch salt
¼ tsp shrimp paste, toasted
¼ bird's eye chilli
2 tsp tamarind pulp
3 tbsp aren palm sugar
50 ml water

Dressing
2 tsp Basa Gede (see page 107)
2 tbsp Rujak Sauce (recipe above)
2 tsp lemon juice
salt, to taste

Exotic Fruits
3 tbsp Langoustine Stock (recipe above)
1 tsp Spiced Syrup (recipe above)
1 tsp coriander seeds (from Spiced Syrup)
1 tsp Fennel Purée (recipe above)
1 tbsp papaya, cut into ½ x ½ cm cubes
1 tbsp pineapple, cut into ½ x ½ cm cubes
1 tbsp snake fruit (salak), cut into ½ x ½ cm cubes
1 tbsp mango, cut into ½ x ½ cm cubes
salt and white pepper, to taste
½ lemon, juice only
½ tsp coriander leaves, chopped

Garnish
4 tbsp micro-coriander (½ punnet)

METHOD

Make the syrup in advance. Put all the ingredients in a saucepan. Bring it to the boil then remove it from the heat. Cool to room temperature, then refrigerate for a minimum of 2 hours.

For the langoustines, remove the heads and shells and set them aside for the stock. Steam the mushroom slices for 1 minute, then pat them dry with paper towels and refrigerate. Lay a piece of cling film on your kitchen countertop. Arrange 3 slices of mushroom close together to form a tight square, with no space between them. Season the langoustine tails with salt and pepper, and drag the point of a toothpick along the underside centre of each langoustine to keep it nice and straight during cooking. Place a langoustine tail horizontally across the mushroom square. Bring the cling film up and over the ingredients and roll tightly with firm pressure. Repeat with the remaining cèpe slices and langoustines, wrapping each one separately in a new piece of cling film. Refrigerate.

To make the stock, clean the langoustine heads and shells by rinsing them under cold water. Roast them in a 200–220°C oven until the shells turn bright orange and a little brown at the edges. Then place the roasted shells in a saucepan with the water and salt, and gently simmer for 45 minutes. Remove from the heat and allow it to cool to room temperature. Strain. Reduce the stock until you get a strong but pleasant langoustine flavour. Season to taste with salt and pepper.

To prepare the purée, cut the fennel bulb into small but regular pieces and steam (or boil) them until they are very soft. Cool them in an ice bath (made with ice cubes and water). Place the cold fennel pieces in a strainer and allow them to drain for a minimum of 30 minutes. Blend the fennel to a fine purée, then strain and refrigerate.

To make the rujak sauce, grind the salt, shrimp paste and chilli with a mortar and pestle. Mix the tamarind pulp, palm sugar and water together in a bowl and massage the mixture by hand until the solids dissolve. Strain. Pour it into the mortar and mix well. Adjust the consistency with hot water to obtain a smooth sauce and set aside.

For the dressing, combine all the ingredients and adjust the seasoning.

To prepare the fruit, combine the langoustine stock with the spiced syrup and fennel purée in a bowl and mix well. Add the diced fruit and coriander seeds. Season to taste with salt, pepper and lemon juice. Stir in the coriander leaves.

To assemble, take the langoustine tails from the refrigerator and discard the cling film. Heat the oil in a pan and sear the langoustines, making sure to sear the side where the mushroom pieces are folded. This prevents the mushrooms from separating from the langoustines. Once they are golden-brown, flip the langoustines over and sear the other side as well. Remove the pan from the heat and add the butter, shallots and thyme. Baste the langoustines with the butter for approximately 1 minute, but don't overcook (they should remain nice and glossy). Drain the langoustines on paper towels, then slice each langoustine into 2 pieces, leaving the tail intact. Decorate the plates with the dressing. Arrange 3 pieces of langoustine on each plate. Top each piece with some fruit, a pinch of sea salt and a few sprigs of micro-coriander leaves. Serve immediately.

TIPS

The choice of fruit in this recipe is flexible, depending on what is available and in season. More importantly, think about mixing fruits of different texture (crunchy, soft, etc), flavour (sweet, sour, etc) and colour.

Rujak sauce is very potent and not for everyone. If you enjoy it, add some shrimp paste and more chilli by all means. If your palate is milder, tone down the taste by leaving out the chilli altogether.

Try drizzling the dressing on lettuce or a salad. It's a stunning combination.

LIMES: KAFFIR, KALAMANSI AND LEMO

Many of Indonesia's islands have their own varieties of citrus fruits. Of the various limes that Mozaic uses, three are featured in the recipes in this book: kaffir lime, *Citrus hystrix Candolle* (Indonesian: *jeruk purut*, Malay: *limau purut*, Thai: *ma kruut*); kalamansi lime, *Citrus x microcarpa* (*Rutaceae*) (Indonesian: *jeruk kasturi,* Malay: *limau kasturi*), and Balinese lemo lime.

FOOD CHARACTER

Kaffir limes have a bright, penetrating lemon-like aroma. The flesh and juice are very sour and slightly bitter. The rind, which carries the aroma and flavour, must be very carefully grated to avoid the bitterness. The leaves are aromatic, dark green and quite thick, which makes them ideal for cooking and stewing. Kalamansi limes have a lemon-tangerine taste that is both sweet and sour. The lemo lime (often mistakenly referred to as a kaffir lime) is a very small, aromatic citrus with an intensely perfumed and slightly peppery flavour.

PHYSICALS

The small kaffir lime tree is often grown in household gardens and bears small, round dark green fruits distinguished by their wrinkly skin and waxy, winged petioles (hourglass-shaped leaves). The kalamansi lime is a hybrid citrus with small and very juicy fruit with bright orange, thin, shiny skins; its leaves aren't used in cooking. Kalamansi limes grow from mid-August to October. The lemo lime, unique to Bali, grows on a small, thorny tree and is often cultivated in household gardens. It has large seeds and thick skin relative to its tiny size. Like kaffir limes, the leaves have winged petioles but of unequal size, with the smaller being on the extremity. Unlike the kaffir lime, the leaves are thin and tender, which makes them ideal for using in raw preparations where the leaves will be eaten raw.

LOCAL USE

The kaffir lime is a key ingredient in Thai cooking. In Indonesia, it is used as a brightening aromatic in peanut-based *pecel* and *gado-gado* sauces. Kalamansi limes aren't readily available in Bali, but they are used in the northern parts of Indonesia in spicy *sambal* condiments, or juiced directly over fish or shellfish. Finely sliced lemo lime leaves (*don lemo*) are an important ingredient in *sambal matah* and salad dishes that call for coconut, such as *urap* and *lawar*.

NOTES FROM CHEF SALANS

We have been able to gather these lime species in Bali and grow enough to make seasonal use of them. In the following recipes, you will see how we use kaffir and kalamansi limes. Lemo limes are used in other recipes throughout the book.

Selecting the ingredient: Limes should be plump with no bruises and have a strong, uniform colour. Lemo and kaffir limes should be dark green. The kalamansi should be the orange of a tangerine or clementine. Leaves should be fresh, dark and uniform in colour.

How to prepare it: Use a microplane to collect the zest, to avoid grating the bitter white flesh beneath the skin. When using the leaves for cooking, wash or simply wipe them before use. The leaves can be infused or bruised, and tossed into the preparation. When using the leaves raw, they must be cut into extremely thin slices, or chopped very finely.

Substitutes: Some lime juices are available frozen, often in professional pastry shops. Frozen leaves are a very poor substitute for fresh leaves. Lemo limes and leaves can be substituted with kaffir limes. Kalamansi limes could be replaced with a mixture of lime juice and mandarin or clementine juice (at a ratio of 50 50), though it would lose its unique taste.

OPPOSITE Kaffir limes (above left), lemo limes (right) and kalamansi limes (below).
THIS PAGE The leaves, juice, flesh and zest of limes can be prepared in many different ways.

kalamansi sorbet with vanilla risotto and pineapple confit

ABOUT THE RECIPE: There are many types of limes in Indonesia, and it can be a real challenge finding out where they grow. There are officially three native limes in Bali, but if you travel 100 km in any direction, you will discover three or more different varieties. When I travelled to Ambon in northern Indonesia, I discovered an amazing lime served in a *sambal* with grilled fish. The cook couldn't give me its name, but I found it similar to the kalamansi limes found in Singapore and Malaysia. It's half lime and half mandarin – the perfect balance between sour and sweet. I immediately asked the cook to send me a few boxes of them each time they come into season. In this recipe, I add fresh tangerine juice to kalamansi juice to adjust its balance of sweet and sour. We then pair the resulting sorbet with various ingredients that balance its intense flavours. A creamy, sweet risotto tones the dish down and gives it a nice texture, and the pepper-pineapple confit adds a kick to the dish as well as a subtle sweetness.

*Elements of this recipe should be prepared 1 day in advance.

PORTION: Serves 10 **DIFFICULTY LEVEL:**

INGREDIENTS

Pineapple Confit

30 g coriander seeds
35 cm cassia bark, broken into pieces
1 vanilla bean, split and seeds scraped
30 star anise, whole
½ orange, zest only, peeled
1 lemon, zest only, peeled
4 sprigs mint
1 litre water
500 g sugar
1½ tbsp black peppercorns
½ pineapple, cut into ½ x ½ x 2 cm sticks

Sorbet

50 g liquid glucose
120 g sugar
3 tbsp water
150 ml milk
⅓ leaf gelatine, pre-soaked
170 ml fresh kalamansi lime juice (use frozen juice if unavailable, such as Boiron brand)
50 ml Balinese tangerine juice (use regular tangerine juice if unavailable)

Pineapple Chips

200 g sugar
200 g (not ml) water
10 or 20 slices pineapple, peeled, 1 mm thick

Pastry Cream

50 ml milk
½ vanilla bean, split and seeds scraped
½ egg yolk
1 tbsp sugar
1 tbsp cake flour

Risotto

3 tbsp risotto rice, uncooked, (such as arborio or carnaroli)
5 g butter, unsalted
150–200 ml milk
½ vanilla bean, seeds scraped
1½ tbsp sugar
1½ tbsp cream
1 quantity of Pastry Cream (recipe above)
75 ml cream, whipped

Condiments and Garnishes

1 tsp black pepper, freshly ground
10 basil leaves, sliced
10 basil tips

Special Equipment

ice cream machine

METHOD

Make the pineapple confit in advance. Dry roast the coriander seeds in a pan until they are fragrant. Then place them in a cheesecloth along with the cassia bark, vanilla bean (seeds and pod), star anise, orange and lemon zest, and mint. Tie the cheesecloth in a bundle so the spices can't escape, and put it in a saucepan with the water and sugar. Bring to the boil. Meanwhile, dry roast the black peppercorns in a pan until they are fragrant. Crush them lightly; each should broken into no more than 3 or 4 pieces. Add these to the saucepan along with the pineapple. Bring everything back to the boil, then remove the saucepan from the heat. Cool to room temperature, then refrigerate for a minimum of 12 hours.

To make the sorbet, bring the glucose, sugar, water and milk to the boil. Remove from the heat and add the gelatine and stir until it has dissolved. Allow to cool to room temperature, then add the juices. Mix well and refrigerate until chilled, then churn in an ice cream machine. Transfer to a plastic container and freeze.

To make the pineapple chips, preheat the oven to 80°C. Bring the sugar and water to the boil, stirring to dissolve the sugar. Remove the pan from the heat and add the pineapple slices, stirring to ensure all the slices are evenly coated with syrup. Remove the slices from the syrup and drain them on paper towels. Arrange the slices on a baking tray lined with a non-stick mat or baking paper and bake for 2–3 hours, or until dry and crispy. Allow to cool to room temperature and store in an airtight container.

To make the pastry cream, bring the milk and vanilla (seeds and pod) to the boil. Meanwhile, thoroughly combine the egg yolk, sugar and flour. Wait for the milk to cool to approximately 85°C, then pour half over the egg mixture. Mix well then pour the mixture into the remaining hot milk. Return to the heat and boil for 2 minutes, stirring continuously with a whisk to make sure it doesn't burn. Pour the mixture into a container and allow it to cool to room temperature, then refrigerate.

To make the risotto, sauté the rice in the butter for 1 minute. Add the vanilla seeds and one third of the milk. Stir continuously until the milk has been absorbed. Repeat with the other two thirds, using more milk if needed. The rice should be soft, not al dente like a savoury risotto. Mix in the sugar and pouring cream, simmering until the sugar has dissolved. Refrigerate. When cold, stir the risotto and pastry cream until combined, then gently fold in the whipped cream. The resulting mixture should be creamy and light. Cover and refrigerate.

To serve, place a couple of spoonfuls of risotto in each of the 10 martini glasses. Top with the poached pineapple, plus a little poaching liquid and black pepper. Place a large scoop, or quenelle, of sorbet in each glass. Top with black pepper, basil leaves, a basil tip and 1–2 pineapple chips. Serve immediately.

TIPS

The amount of tangerine juice may need to be adjusted depending on the quality of the kalamansi limes you use. Increase the tangerine juice if your kalamansi limes are very sour. Dispense with the tangerine juice if your kalamansis are ripe and perfectly balanced.

For information on simple syrups, setting very low oven temperatures and how to make sorbet if you don't have an ice cream machine, see Techniques (page 140).

barramundi confit with kaffir gelée, kaffir lime dressing and shaved fennel salad

ABOUT THE RECIPE: Here is a typical Mozaic recipe that achieves a perfect balance between the influences of the East and West. The kaffir lime offers a heady aroma that no other lime can match, but unfortunately, it's very bitter. In Indonesian cooking, the leaf is primarily used, but we wanted to focus on the lime itself because of its amazing fragrance. We developed a dressing with a sweet base that would not only counteract the bitterness of the lime, but also allow us to introduce a subtle flavour – a local flower honey. We have some wonderful varieties of honey in Bali, and when we combined the two flavours, the fusion was perfect – and so versatile. Paired with a crunchy fennel salad and good quality caviar, this dish is a real talking point among Mozaic diners.

PORTION: Serves 6 as an appetiser or 3 as a main course

DIFFICULTY LEVEL:

INGREDIENTS

Toasted Almonds
30 g sliced almonds
1 tbsp egg white
1 tsp andaliman pepper, coarsely ground
½ tsp white peppercorn, coarsely ground
2 tsp kaffir lime zest, finely grated
¼ tsp salt
2 tbsp brown sugar

Kaffir Dressing
1½ tbsp good quality honey
2 tbsp kaffir lime juice
100 ml salad oil
1 tsp kaffir lime zest, finely grated
salt and white pepper, to taste

Jelly
orange zest, peeled (to make 2 tsp purée)
75 ml orange juice, freshly squeezed
3 tsp sugar
14 kaffir lime leaves, roughly chopped
3 tbsp kaffir lime juice
1 tsp plain konnyaku jelly powder (Nutrijell or any other quality brand)
1 tbsp olive oil
kaffir lime salt, to taste, see Techniques (page 140)

Fish
480 g barramundi fillets, 6 x 80 g or 3 x 160 g portions
salt and white pepper, to taste
olive oil, as needed
6 kaffir lime leaves, bruised
kaffir lime salt, to taste

Fennel Salad
60 g fennel, peeled and finely shaved
6 mint leaves, finely sliced
2 kaffir lime leaves, finely sliced
1 tbsp Toasted Almonds, crushed (recipe above)
2 tbsp Kaffir Dressing (recipe above)
kaffir lime salt, to taste
white pepper, freshly ground to taste

Condiments and Garnishes
6 tsp caviar
6 fresh herb sprigs of your choice

METHOD

For the almonds, mix all the ingredients together and bake in a 130°C oven for 25–30 minutes or until golden-brown. Cool to room temperature and store in an airtight container.

To make the dressing, whisk the honey and lime juice together. Continue whisking and gradually add the salad oil until you have a smooth and thick dressing. Once it's combined, add the zest and adjust the seasoning.

To make the jelly, cover the orange zest with water and bring it to the boil. Strain and rinse thoroughly. Repeat twice then blend the zest in a mini food processor until it's smooth. Bring the orange juice and sugar to the boil, then add the lime leaves. Cover, set aside and allow to infuse for 15–20 minutes. Strain. Add the blended orange zest, lime juice and konnyaku jelly powder, and return to the heat. Boil for 1 minute, stirring continuously. Pour into a container so the liquid reaches a depth of 1 cm. Allow to set at room temperature then refrigerate. Cut into 1 x 1 cm cubes and set aside.

At least 1 hour before serving, prepare the fish. Preheat the oven to 50°C. Season the fillets then place them in an ovenproof dish in a single layer, with some space between them so that the fillets don't stick together. Add enough olive oil to cover the fish by at least 1 cm. Bruise the lime leaves and put them in the oil with the fish. Place the tray in the oven and cook for approximately 45 minutes. When ready, the fish should look undercooked but break apart easily when pressed with a fork. Remove the tray from the oven and take the fish from the oil, draining it on paper towels. Season with sea salt.

Meanwhile, season 12 cubes of jelly to taste with kaffir lime salt and olive oil.

Prepare the salad by combining all the ingredients and adjusting the seasoning.

Using a spoon, place 1½ tbsp of dressing in the centre of each plate and make a circle with the dressing.

Reheat the confied fish in a 140°C oven for no more than 1 minute (so that it retains its beautiful colour and texture). Place a piece of fish in the centre of the dressing. Top the fish with the fennel salad. Garnish each salad with a tsp of caviar and a fresh herb sprig. Serve immediately.

TIPS

To juice kaffir limes, I let the fruit ripen until it turns yellow. It yields 10 times the amount of juice, and has a much better flavour than the juice from green kaffir limes.

For more information on setting very low oven temperatures, see Techniques (page 140).

Grated kaffir lime zest (top), Balinese sea salt (middle) and kaffir lime salt (bottom).

NUTMEG AND MACE

NUTMEG
Myristica fragrans (*Myristicaceae*)
Indonesian: *pala*
Balinese: *jibug arum*

MACE
Myristicae arillus
Indonesian: *fuli*

FOOD CHARACTER

Nutmeg and the more delicately flavoured mace are aromatic staples of the Western pastry tradition, but, interestingly, they also add intriguing notes to savoury dishes. Nutmeg's characteristic aroma has a trace of heat, while mace imparts something of its red colouring and is a bit sweeter and more intense. Mace is also popular dried and candied.

PHYSICALS

Nutmeg and mace are two spices from the fruit of the nutmeg tree, which is indigenous to the Banda islands of eastern Indonesia. What is called nutmeg is the seed itself, while mace is the aril, a lacy, leathery covering between the fruit and the seed. The nutmeg kernel is encased in a shiny, dark shell. In Indonesia, the fleshy and very sour fruit (pericarp) is used, amongst other things, to make a jam.

LOCAL USE

Nutmeg is part of the Balinese spice palette and pharmacopoeia. It's sometimes added to the spice mix called basa gede.

NOTES FROM CHEF SALANS

Nutmeg in Indonesia is wonderful. One can get extremely fresh nutmeg, which is unlike any nutmeg I have ever used. People here simply crush the whole nutmeg and throw it into the dish to infuse; the flavour is pleasant and not too overpowering. One can also buy the fruit of the nutmeg, which is also available candied and as a jam. In the following recipes, you will learn how to use all three parts of the nutmeg.

Selecting the ingredient: There are two types of nutmeg: one with a rather round shell (from Banda) and one whose shell is more oval (from Madagascar). Although both nutmegs are great, the round one is slightly better and more aromatic than the oval one. If you can't find fresh nutmeg, buy nutmeg that is still in its shell: you will need to crack the shell open and remove the nutmeg kernel inside. For mace, try to select the whole mace and one that is a bright, intense red.

How to prepare it: If you have access to fresh nutmeg and mace, simply crack or bruise it and add the whole nutmeg to your preparation in the last few minutes of cooking (this is how it's done in the Banda islands). With dried nutmeg and mace, the flavour is much more intense and therefore less of it is needed. For this reason, it's often used at the beginning of the cooking process so that it can infuse slowly into the food.

Substitutes: Fresh nutmeg and mace can be substituted with dried products, but I'd cut the quantities approximately by half. Ground nutmeg may smell and taste great the first time, but once the container is opened, the quality will start to deteriorate as the spice's volatile oils are exposed to oxygen. It's better to grate a nutmeg kernel as and when you need it. There is no substitute for candied nutmeg fruit, but you could try to make the recipe with another candied hard fruit, such as quince.

OPPOSITE The whole nutmeg fruit, with the white pericarp and the red mace aril wrapped around the nutmeg kernel.
THIS PAGE The nutmeg kernel in its shell, hulled and grated (left) and mace on the kernel, removed from the kernel, and chopped (right).

nutmeg sorbet with snake fruit confit and sprite-kaffir leaf emulsion

ABOUT THE RECIPE: In this dish, we use the seed of the nutmeg fruit, as well as its red "lacy" covering known as mace. Both are highly aromatic, so they need to be used carefully. We used the two spices to create a sorbet – sweet and refreshing, yet fragrant and potent. Married with yet another magical Balinese ingredient, the snake fruit (salak), the dish is a perfect balance of flavours. Now, snake fruit is one of those fruit that doesn't have universal appeal. Quite a few people are repelled by its floury texture. However, we discovered that when poached properly, it loses that flouriness but retains its crunchy bite. As for the addition of Sprite, I had heard about chicken served in Coca-Cola sauce, so I thought: Why not do a Sprite-based dish? The fizzy, citrusy beverage not only helps to pull together all the flavours of the dish, it also adds a hint of bubbly fun.

PORTION: Serves 10 **DIFFICULTY LEVEL:**

INGREDIENTS

Sorbet
250 ml water
50 g sugar
70 g liquid glucose
2 tsp whole nutmeg, crushed
2 tbsp whole mace
14 cm cassia bark
4 large sage leaves
1 leaf gelatine, pre-soaked
100 g plain yoghurt, unsweetened
2 tbsp lemon juice

Snake Fruit Confit
500 ml water
250 g sugar
50 cm cassia bark
15 star anise, whole
300 g snake fruit (salak), peeled, deseeded and sliced
½ vanilla bean, split in half
3 tbsp lemon juice

Emulsion
3 tbsp water
1 tbsp sugar
40 kaffir lime leaves, sliced
80 ml Sprite
¼ tsp soya lecithin powder (or more if needed)

Black Rice Tuile
120 g Black Rice Porridge (see page 61)
2½ tbsp glutinous rice flour
1 tsp cocoa powder
3½ tbsp white sugar

Garnish
10 fresh herb sprigs of your choice

Special Equipment
ice cream machine

METHOD

To prepare the sorbet, bring the water, sugar and glucose to the boil. Add the nutmeg, mace, cassia bark and sage. Remove from the heat, cover with a lid and allow it to infuse for 1 hour. Strain. Reheat 50 ml of the liquid in another saucepan, then add the gelatine and stir until it dissolves. Add this mixture back into the rest of the liquid. Whisk in the yoghurt and lemon juice. Mix until smooth and chill in the refrigerator. Churn the sorbet in an ice cream machine until it hardens. Transfer it to a plastic container and freeze.

To prepare the snake fruit, bring the water, sugar, cassia bark, vanilla bean and star anise to the boil. Add the snake fruit and allow it to simmer until it's just past al dente (it shouldn't be too soft). Remove it from heat and pour the confit and syrup into a container. Let it to cool to room temperature. By the time the syrup has cooled, the snake fruit should be well cooked but not mushy. Add the lemon juice. Refrigerate.

For the emulsion, bring the water and sugar to the boil. Add the lime leaves, cover with a lid, remove from the heat and allow it to infuse for 20 minutes. Strain and allow it to cool to room temperature. Add the Sprite and soya lecithin, and blend the liquid with a hand blender to develop a strong foam. Add more soya lecithin if needed. Set aside.

To make the tuile, preheat the oven to 110°C. Blend all the ingredients in a processor until smooth. Strain. Place spoonfuls of batter on a non-stick mat or baking paper and spread each one with a spoon into circles that are 1 mm thick and 7–8 cm in diameter. Bake for 15 minutes. Flip the tuile and bake for 1 hour, or until crispy. Remove the tray from the oven and allow the tuiles to cool before storing them in an airtight container.

Divide the snake fruit confit among 10 martini glasses. Pour some poaching liquid into each glass so the snake fruit is covered. Place a scoop, or quenelle, of sorbet in each glass. Top with some foam from the emulsion, a tuile and a fresh herb sprig. Serve immediately.

TIPS

Always opt for fresh nutmeg and mace whenever possible. Dried versions won't taste as good.

For more information on how to make sorbet if you don't have an ice cream machine, see Techniques (page 140).

pan-seared foie gras with apple, saffron and nutmeg purée

ABOUT THE RECIPE: Have you ever tasted nutmeg and saffron together? It's a heavenly combination. I inhaled their aromas often in the markets on the Banda islands in Maluku province, where fresh nutmeg and saffron grown there are sold. I wanted to recreate the magic of that smell, so we combined both saffron and nutmeg jam from the Banda islands with something milder – apples – to create a delicately spiced marmalade. We then paired this with tamarind to create a dish with a perfect balance of sweetness and sourness. The addition of foie gras, with its rich, creamy texture (which I have a certain weakness for) fits beautifully with the sweet and sour flavours in this deliciously simple dish.

*Elements of this recipe should be prepared 1 day in advance.

PORTION: Serves 6 as an appetiser or 3 as a main **DIFFICULTY LEVEL:**

INGREDIENTS

Apple Purée
200 g cooking apples, peeled, cored and diced
25 threads saffron (Iranian or Spanish, if possible)
1 tbsp nutmeg jam
salt and white pepper, to taste

Foie Gras
6 slices foie gras, grade A, 60 g each (or 3 x 120 g)
salt and white pepper, to taste
6 tbsp shallots, sliced
1 tsp thyme leaves
3 tbsp candied nutmeg fruit, finely sliced
sea salt, to taste

Tamarind Demi-Glaçe
1 tbsp tamarind pulp
3 tbsp water
100 ml beef demi-glaçe, see Techniques (page 140)
salt and white pepper, to taste

Condiments and Garnishes
6 fresh herb sprigs of your choice
6 tbsp Rujak Sauce (see page 113)

METHOD

Make the apple purée in advance. Place the apples in a saucepan. Cover and cook over medium heat until the apples are soft. Add the saffron and nutmeg jam. Mix well. Adjust the seasoning. Refrigerate and allow the apples to marinate for a minimum of 12 hours.

Season the foie gras slices with salt and pepper. Sauté them over medium to high heat until golden-brown on both sides. Reduce the heat slightly and continue cooking until the centre of the foie gras is warm to the touch. Reduce the heat to low and move the foie gras to the side of the pan. Add the shallots, thyme and nutmeg fruit. Cook gently for a minute until the shallots turn translucent. Remove the foie gras, nutmeg fruit and shallots from the pan and drain them on paper towels. Season with sea salt. Reserve the fat in the pan for the sauce.

To prepare the demi-glaçe, massage the tamarind pulp in water until it dissolves, then strain. Deglaze the foie gras pan with the demi-glaçe. Reduce the demi-glaçe to a syrupy consistency and season to taste with salt and pepper. Adjust the acidity of the sauce with tamarind water to taste.

Reheat the apple purée. Drizzle a ring of rujak sauce on each pre-warmed plate. Spoon some apple purée into the centre of each ring, and top it with a slice of foie gras. Drizzle some demi-glaçe over it, and garnish it with a fresh herb sprig. Serve immediately.

TIP

If nutmeg jam and candied fruit are unavailable, or if you don't have time to make your own, you may substitute it with guava jam and pieces of candied guava, or quince jam and candied quince.

PALM SUGAR

AREN PALM SUGAR

From the palm *Arenga pinnata* (*Wurmb.*) *Merr.* (*Arecaceae*)
Indonesian: *gula aren*, *gula merah*, *gula jawa*
Balinese: *gula bali* (from the tree called *taru jaka*)
Also known as: palm sugar, enau sugar, red sugar

COCONUT PALM SUGAR

From the palm *Cocos nucifera, Linn.* (*Arecaceae*)
Indonesian: *gula kelapa*
Balinese: *gula nyuh*

FOOD CHARACTER

Aren palm sugar is mildly sweet, with a smoky, slightly molasses-like flavour that adds richness and depth of colour to savoury dishes without undue sweetness, and combines well with tamarind, shrimp paste and chillies. In sweet dishes, it's often boiled into a syrup with a characteristic dark, smoky flavour. Coconut palm sugar is a blonde sugar with characteristic palm sugar sweetness and a trace of coconut. When coconut palm sugar is produced from pure coconut sap and not mixed with other sugars, it has been shown to have exceptional nutritional properties and is very low on the glycaemic index. This has made it a subject of interest among doctors and researchers, and it's gaining popularity among sugar-conscious consumers.

PHYSICALS

Aren palm sugar is the lightly processed nectar of the *Arenga pinnata* palm. The sap (*air nipa*) is harvested, boiled for hours and allowed to thicken, then made into small, reddish-brown, semi-spherical or cylindrical cakes. One aren palm tree yields about 8 litres of *air nipa* daily, which can produce 1.5 kg of palm sugar. Coconut palm sugar is produced in much the same manner. It has a lighter colour and can sometimes be quite pale; it also has a lower moisture content that makes it easy to turn it into granules or powder.

LOCAL USE

Indonesians use both aren palm sugar (or the nearly identical hard brown sugar made from the palmyra or lontar palm) and coconut palm sugar in traditional cakes, sweet beverages like *cendol*, savoury dishes like *rujak* and in sauces for fish and meat, such as *gulai*. Still cheap compared to refined cane sugar, it was formerly used as a sweetener for coffee. In the old days, people would hold a piece of red sugar between their teeth and sip unsweetened black coffee. This awkward practice has mostly died out, but some old people in the mountains of Bali may still drink coffee this way.

NOTES FROM CHEF SALANS

Both the aren and coconut palm sugars are very interesting ingredients as they can be used as a sugar, but are less sweet than regular white sugar. Aren and coconut palm sugars are thicker after they melt, and can therefore act as a thickening agent in certain recipes. They also add subtle flavours of smokiness and caramel to dishes, and their very high burning point makes them ideal for preparations that require high temperatures.
Selecting the ingredient: Both sugars are best when they are hard and light-coloured (pale brown for coconut palm sugar and brown for aren palm sugar). When the sugars are soft and have a dark colour, they are of lesser quality. Sugars that have been drying out on a shelf for a very long time will appear firm, but the colour will still be dark.
How to prepare it: Aren and coconut palm sugars can be used as they are, shaved off into chips or ground into a powder. They can also be dissolved in hot water to make a syrup, which is used as it is (for example, drizzled over fruits), or in further cooking or other preparations.
Substitutes: These sugars are available in granule or paste form, and also sold in tubes, blocks or cans. In the following recipes, aren and coconut palm sugars can be substituted with other brown sugars; be sure to select a very moist and sticky sugar to replace aren palm sugar, and a dried brown sugar to replace coconut palm sugar.

OPPOSITE Boiled palm sap being poured into coconut shell moulds to make palm sugar.
THIS PAGE Coconut and palm sugar in solid cakes, sliced, powdered and melted.

palm sugar and coffee-marinated wagyu beef tenderloin with mamey sapote purée

ABOUT THE RECIPE: This recipe features more classic ingredients from the Indonesian *terroir*: coconut palm sugar, coffee and mamey sapote. Pairing palm sugar with coffee comes naturally enough; a whiff of the intoxicating air at the local palm sugar refinery at coffee break will convince anyone of how well the two aromas mingle. But I took their relationship to new heights by introducing the exotic mamey sapote to the mix. The spice-inflected flesh of this fruit perfectly complements the flavours of coffee and palm sugar. Although I'm familiar with sapodilla, I discovered its variant, the mamey sapote, only a few years ago. It's an amazing find, considering my years of living in Bali and interest in seeking out new ingredients.

PORTION: Serves 6 as an appetiser **DIFFICULTY LEVEL:** 2 of 3

INGREDIENTS

Beef
500 g wagyu beef tenderloin
2 tbsp coffee beans, roasted and ground
3 tbsp coconut palm sugar
salt and white pepper, to taste
1 tbsp salad oil

Toasted Spices
3 tbsp cubeb peppercorns (use 1 tbsp of regular black peppercorns if unavailable)
2 tbsp coffee beans, roasted
2⅓ tbsp juniper berries
4 tbsp kenari nuts, finely sliced (use almonds if unavailable)
2 tsp orange zest, finely grated
50 g aren palm sugar
50 g coconut palm sugar

Mamey Sapote Purée
250 g mamey sapote, skinned and pitted (use sapodillas if unavailable)
chicken stock, as needed, see Techniques (page 140)
salt and white pepper, to taste

Spinach
35 g butter, unsalted
6 cloves garlic, roasted, see Techniques (page 140)
3 tbsp shallots, chopped
250 g spinach leaves, stems removed
salt and white pepper, to taste

Sauce
30 strips orange zest, julienned
150 ml beef demi-glaçe, see Techniques (page 140)
6 coffee beans, roasted and crushed
salt and black pepper to taste

Garnish
6 fresh herb sprigs of your choice

METHOD

To prepare the tenderloin, mix the ground coffee with the coconut palm sugar, salt and pepper to form a dry paste. Rub the mixture into the meat. Cover with cling film and refrigerate for 1 hour. Rinse the beef to remove the spices and pat dry. Preheat the oven to 200°C. Season with salt and pepper. Heat the oil in a pan and sear the tenderloin until it's brown all over (you may need to cut the tenderloin in half to fit it into the pan). Place the meat in a roasting pan with a wire rack insert and put the pan in the oven. Close the oven door and turn the heat off. Cook the meat in the residual heat for 1–1½ hours; don't open the oven door during this time. The meat should be rare when it comes out of the oven.

Next, prepare the toasted spices. Preheat the oven to 150°C. Using a spice grinder or mortar and pestle, grind the peppercorns and coffee beans coarsely. Gradually add the juniper berries, kenari nuts, orange zest and the 2 types of sugar, and grind them lightly until you have a coarse mixture. Spread the mixture on a baking tray lined with a non-stick mat or baking paper and bake for 15 minutes. The mixture should start to bubble when it's done. Allow it to cool to room temperature before breaking it into small lumps. Store in an airtight container.

For the mamey sapote, purée the fruit in a processor and press it through a fine sieve. Pour the purée into a saucepan and thin it out with chicken stock. Season to taste with salt and pepper. Don't boil the purée as it will lose its delicate taste and texture.

To prepare the spinach, heat a large sauté pan over medium heat and lightly brown the butter. Add the shallots and garlic. Remove from the heat and add the spinach. Toss quickly, allowing the spinach to wilt, but not sear. Season to taste with salt and pepper.

For the sauce, cover the zest with water and bring it to the boil. Strain and rinse thoroughly. Repeat this twice. Bring the beef demi-glaçe to the boil. Add the coffee beans, cover with a lid and allow to infuse for 10 minutes. Add the orange zest strips and season to taste with salt and pepper. Set aside.

Remove the beef from the oven and slice it. Season to taste with salt and pepper, and reheat it in a 180°C oven until the meat is done to your liking. Meanwhile, reheat the purée, spinach and sauce. Put a spoonful of purée on one side of each plate and drag the spoon through it to the other side to create a line of purée. Put a small mound of spinach on one side of the line and top it with the tenderloin slices, then pour a spoonful of sauce over the beef. Garnish with a sprinkling of toasted spices and a fresh herb sprig.

TIP

Mamey sapote is not an easy ingredient to pin down; you can substitute it with a purée of pumpkin roasted with brown sugar, star anise and ground nutmeg.

turmeric-chocolate fondant and palm sugar ice cream with asian salad

ABOUT THE RECIPE: Coconut palm sugar is an amazing ingredient. It's extremely versatile and offers many advantages over other types of sugar. In the following recipe, we not only demonstrate different ways of using this sugar (in a cake, sauce and ice cream), but we also infuse spices into it to develop deeper and more intriguing characteristics. The strong flavour of fresh turmeric works nicely with the sweet, smoky, caramelised aroma of the sugar, creating a completely new way to enjoy palm sugar.

PORTION: Serves 10 **DIFFICULTY LEVEL:**

INGREDIENTS

Pastry
125 g butter, unsalted, room temperature
125 g icing sugar
1 whole egg
1 egg yolk
4 tbsp cocoa powder
280 g cake flour

Chocolate Ganache
150 ml cream
75 g dark chocolate, chopped
2 tbsp dark chocolate, melted and used as a glue
3 tbsp butter, for large moulds
3 tbsp cocoa powder, for large moulds

Turmeric Coconut Palm Sugar
10 g fresh turmeric, peeled and grated
150 g coconut palm sugar

Chocolate Fondant
220 g butter, unsalted
260 g dark chocolate, chopped
175 g white sugar
1 pinch salt
2 eggs
½ tsp lime zest, finely grated
1 tbsp vanilla essence
220 g cake flour
2 tbsp cocoa powder
1 tsp baking powder

Turmeric Sauce
200 g fresh coconut cream
50 g Turmeric Coconut Palm Sugar (recipe above)
10 g fresh turmeric, sliced

Ice cream
500 ml milk
3½ tbsp milk powder
50 ml cream
50 g liquid glucose
4 egg yolks
100 g Turmeric Coconut Palm Sugar (recipe above)
½ leaf gelatine, pre-soaked

METHOD

To prepare the pastry, cream the butter and icing sugar until smooth. Add the whole egg and combine, making sure it's fully incorporated. Repeat with the egg yolk. Add the cocoa and flour, mixing until the dough comes together. Form a ball with the dough, cover it with cling film and allow it to rest in the refrigerator for 30 minutes. Preheat the oven to 140°C. When the dough has rested, roll it out to a thickness of 2 mm. Use the large mould or a cutter to cut out 10 x 6 cm circles of pastry. Place the pastry circles on a tray lined with non-stick mat or baking paper and bake the pastries for 14–16 minutes or until light brown. Cool to room temperature and store in an airtight container.

To prepare the ganache, bring the cream to the boil. Pour it over the chocolate in a mixing bowl. Stir the mixture until the chocolate has melted and the mixture is smooth. Pour the mixture into the small PVC moulds and freeze.

Next, prepare the stainless-steel moulds. Use a pastry brush to coat the inside of each mould with melted butter. Dust the insides with cocoa, making sure they are evenly coated. Refrigerate the moulds until the butter has set.

To make the turmeric coconut palm sugar, use your fingers to combine the turmeric with the sugar. Allow the mixture to dry at room temperature, or in a 60–80°C oven for 1 hour, or until dry. Cool to room temperature and store in an airtight container.

Arrange the pastries on a baking tray and fit the large stainless-steel moulds over them. Take the ganaches from the freezer, and remove the PVC moulds. Place a ganache in the centre of each stainless-steel mould, using the melted chocolate to glue the ganache to the pastry. Freeze.

For the fondant, place the butter and chocolate in a mixing bowl over a pan of simmering water to melt the chocolate. Meanwhile, whisk the sugar, salt, eggs, zest and vanilla essence together until smooth. Add the melted chocolate mixture and stir to combine. Sift the flour, cocoa and baking powder together, then gradually add it to the mixture. If you find the mixture is too thick, add some hot water (up to 1 tbsp). Take the stainless-steel moulds from the refrigerator, and pour the fondant mixture into the moulds. The mixture should cover the ganache by at least 1 cm. Refrigerate (or freeze if you are making the fondant ahead of time).

To make the turmeric sauce, bring the coconut cream and turmeric palm sugar to the boil. Add the turmeric, cover with a lid, remove from heat and allow it to infuse for 30 minutes. Strain and set aside.

For the ice cream, bring the milk, milk powder, cream and glucose to the boil in a saucepan. Meanwhile, beat the egg yolks and turmeric palm sugar together in a bowl until the mixture turns pale. Pour a little of the milk mixture into the egg mixture and stir well, then transfer it into the saucepan containing the remaining milk mixture. Cook it slowly over low heat, stirring continuously with a wooden or plastic spoon. When the mixture starts to coat the spoon, remove it from heat. Add the gelatine and stir to dissolve. Fill a big bowl with ice and place a saucepan in it. Strain the mixture into the saucepan and allow it to cool in the refrigerator. When it's cold, churn it in an ice cream machine until it hardens. Transfer it to a plastic container and freeze.

Coriander Caramel
½ tsp coriander seeds
50 g white sugar
2 tbsp water
2 tbsp white wine vinegar

Chilli Confit
2 tbsp Lombok chillies (or red chillies), julienned
50 g sugar
50 g (not ml) water

Asian Salad
4 tbsp pineapple, cut into strips
4 tbsp mango, diced
4 tbsp snake fruit (salak), cut in wedges
4 tbsp mangosteen, scrape flesh off seeds
4 tbsp banana, diced
1 tbsp Chilli Confit, without syrup (recipe above)
1 tbsp coriander leaves, finely sliced
3 tbsp Coriander Caramel (recipe above)

Garnish
10 fresh herb sprigs of your choice

Special Equipment
ice cream machine
10 PVC moulds, 2 cm wide x 3 cm tall*
10 stainless-steel moulds, 6 cm wide x 4½ cm tall

* It's fine to use different-sized moulds, but one should always be half the size of the other, and be able to fit inside it. If commercial moulds are not available, they can be made using PVC pipe.

To make the caramel, dry roast the coriander seeds in a pan until they are fragrant. Set aside. Stir the sugar over medium heat in the same pan until it melts and caramelises (approximately 5 minutes). Remove from the heat and add the water. Stir until the caramel dissolves. Allow it to cool a little. Place the caramel and coriander seeds in a blender and blend until the mixture is smooth. Thin out the caramel mixture with the white wine vinegar

For the chilli confit, put the chilli, sugar and water in a saucepan and simmer very gently until the liquid becomes a thick syrup. Taste one of the chilli strips; it should be tender and sweet. If not, add more water and continue to cook it slowly When they are ready, remove the saucepan from the heat and allow it to cool to room temperature. Refrigerate.

For the salad, toss all the ingredients together and refrigerate.

Preheat the oven to 180°C. Bake the fondant for 8–10 minutes (13–15 minutes for frozen fondants) until the centre of the fondant is lukewarm, but still liquid.

Put a spoonful of turmeric sauce in the centre of each plate, shape it into a circle and place a fondant on top. Place a small mound of salad and a large scoop, or quenelle, of ice cream on the side. Garnish the fondant with a fresh herb sprig. Serve immediately.

TIPS

Try infusing brown sugar with turmeric or other spices, such as ginger, galangal and lemongrass. It yields truly amazing results, and will inspire you to greater levels of culinary experimentation.

For information on simple syrups, making a caramel and how to make ice cream if you don't have an ice cream machine, see Techniques (page 140).

DURIAN

Durio zibethinus (*Malvaceae*)
Indonesian: durian
Balinese: *durèn*

FOOD CHARACTER

Durian is a large, heavy fruit with an infamously penetrating odour that has been described variously as "roasted almonds" and "used surgical swabs"; many also discern a trace of onions and turpentine. Its custard-like flesh is rich, creamy and complex. Southeast Asians are passionately fond of durian, but are forbidden to take the fruit into public buildings (and on the subway in Singapore) in the interest of common courtesy.

PHYSICALS

Durian is native to Indonesia and Malaysia. There are 30 species of the *durio* tree, which produce edible fruit and hundreds of durian cultivars. The tree grows to a height of 25–50 metres, with fruit weighing 1–3 kg. In Bali, the durian season is in December. Durians have spiky husks and pods of edible flesh encasing large seeds; the latter are edible, but only when cooked.

LOCAL USE

According to the Balinese, the ideal circumstance for eating durian is when a ripe fruit falls from the tree and lands in front of you. The fruit continues to ripen for several days after harvesting and must be consumed fresh. In Java, the seeds are sliced finely and cooked in sugar as a sweet snack.

NOTES FROM CHEF SALANS

Knowing that restaurants and hotels in Asia don't allow durian to be brought in because of its stench, I just had to break the rules and bring durian to the Mozaic table. We came up with several recipes featuring durian, two of which are presented here. These are wonderful introductions to durian. Durian addicts will be able to consume three times more durian than we use in our recipes – they will enjoy the durian mousse. Novices might begin with the durian and chocolate mix.

Selecting the ingredient: Unless you have grown up with durian or eat it regularly, it's hard to know how to select it. I've found that it's a matter of looks, smell and the sound it makes when you tap on the fruit – a hollow sound indicates that the fruit is damaged or not ripe. Choose durian with no bruises or insect holes. Make sure that its smell is evident from far away but it's not overly ripe or starting to ferment (unless that is the way you like it).

How to prepare it: Cut open the skin at the bottom of the durian with a knife or sharp tool, break the shell apart and tear it off. Remove the bulbs of fruit, discarding any that are mouldy, spoiled or fermented. Remove the flesh from the seeds before use.

Substitutes: There is no substitute for durian. However, durian paste is sometimes available in Asian food stores. It doesn't taste much like the fresh fruit, since it has been processed and cooked with sugar, but it could be worth a try if you want to make a cautious acquaintance with this fruit.

OPPOSITE The spiky and famously smelly durian fruit, as one might find them in a market.
THIS PAGE The flesh of the opened durian, with its seeds and bulbs of flesh.

durian mousse with jackfruit sorbet, milk crisps and cassia emulsion

ABOUT THE RECIPE: Durian is adored by Asian cultures and rebuffed by the rest of the world; this "delicacy" is like a nice strong cheese to the French. Being French, I couldn't think of a reason why I should enjoy an Epoisse but not a durian, so I tried it. Sure enough, it was horrible, as the fruit I had bitten into was overripe and fermented. Several years later, I met my wife and, as she adored durian, I agreed to give it another try. It was then I discovered that not all durians are awful. I started off trying the ones that were slightly underripe. Then I moved on to riper and riper fruit until I was eating the real thing. Although I like the flavour now, I can't eat a lot of it; durian remains on the palate and in the stomach for quite some time. Now I understand what the local saying, "it makes you hot inside" means. In this particular recipe, durian is served cold and paired with jackfruit, which is another strong-tasting (but much less intense) fruit. The two aromas balance each other out nicely.

*Elements of this recipe should be prepared 1 day in advance.

PORTION: Serves 10 **DIFFICULTY LEVEL:** 🍴🍴🍴

INGREDIENTS

Emulsion
1 litre water
30 cm cassia bark
⅛ orange, zest only, peeled
½ vanilla bean, split, seeds retained
1⅓ tbsp white sugar
¼ tsp soya lecithin powder (or more if needed)

Crisps
120 g white rice, steamed
2¼ tbsp glutinous rice flour
3½ tbsp milk powder
3½ tbsp sugar
1 tsp lime zest, finely grated

Candied Orange Peel
2 oranges, skin only
75 g sugar
75 g (not ml) water

Mousse
90 ml cream (reserve 10 tsp for garnish)
1 tsp sugar
½ leaf gelatine, pre-soaked
75 g durian, strained

Jackfruit Sauce
250 g ripe jackfruit
2 tsp sugar
150 ml water
1 tsp lemon juice

Sorbet
250 g jackfruit, blend in a processor, then a blender
2 tsp sugar
150 ml water
2 tsp lemon juice
1 leaf gelatine, pre-soaked

Orange Sauce
4 oranges, zest only, peeled
3 tbsp water

Jelly
orange zest, peeled (to make 4 tbsp of purée)
3 tbsp water
½ tsp plain konnyaku jelly powder (Nutrijell or any other quality brand)
1 pinch salt

Garnishes
20 strips Candied Orange Peel (recipe above)
20 strips jackfruit, cut into strips
10 herb tips of your choice
10 tsp whipped cream (reserved from mousse)

Special Equipment
ice cream machine

METHOD

Make the emulsion in advance. Boil the cassia bark, zest, vanilla, sugar and water until it has reduced by half. Refrigerate for 24 hours. Strain. Bring to the boil, then add the soya lecithin. Blend the liquid with a hand blender to develop a strong foam. Add more soya lecithin if needed.

To make the crisps, preheat the oven to 110°C. Blend all the ingredients until smooth. Strain. Place spoonfuls of the batter on a non-stick mat or baking paper and spread each one lightly with a spoon into circles that are 1 mm thick and 7–8 cm in diameter. Bake for 15 minutes. Flip and bake for 1 hour or until crispy. Allow to cool to room temperature, then store in an airtight container.

To prepare the candied orange peel, cut the skin (ie, zest and white pith) off the oranges with a sharp knife and set aside the peeled fruit for later use. Cover the skins with water in a saucepan and bring to the boil. Strain and rinse thoroughly. Repeat this process 4 more times. Place the blanched skin, sugar and water in a saucepan over very low heat, and gently simmer until a thick syrup forms. Taste the skin; it should be tender and sweet. If not, add a little water and continue cooking. Remove from the heat and allow it to cool to room temperature. Remove the skins from the syrup and and cut them into ½ cm wide strips. Set aside.

To make the mousse, add a little of the cream to the sugar and stir over medium heat until the sugar has melted. Remove from the heat, add the gelatine and stir to dissolve. Allow the mixture to cool to room temperature, then add it to the whipped cream, gently folding it in. Take a quarter of the mixture and stir it into the durian, then gently fold the remaining cream into the durian mixture. Transfer it to a bowl or container and refrigerate.

To make the jackfruit sauce, blend all the ingredients in a blender until smooth, then strain and set aside.

To make the sorbet, blend the jackfruit, sugar, water and lemon juice until smooth. Strain. Take 50 ml of the mixture and gently heat it, then add the gelatine and stir to dissolve. Add it back into the remaining mixture. Refrigerate until chilled, then churn the sorbet in an ice cream machine until it hardens. Transfer to a plastic container and freeze.

To make the orange sauce, cover the zest with water and bring it to the boil. Strain and rinse thoroughly. Repeat this 3 more times. Blend the blanched orange zest together with the 3 tbsp of water in a food processor. Strain and chill.

To make the jelly, prepare the zest in the same manner as for the orange sauce, blanching it 4 times. You should end up with 35 g of blanched orange zest. Purée the zest with the water and strain. Bring the purée to the boil in a small saucepan, then add the salt and konnyaku jelly powder, whisking continuously to make sure it doesn't burn. Boil for 30 seconds, then pour it into a container so the mixture sits at a depth of 1 cm. Cool to room temperature and cut it into 1 x 1 x 2 cm cubes. Set aside.

To serve, decorate each plate with the orange sauce, jackfruit sauce and 2 orange jellies. Top each jelly with a piece of candied orange peel. Put a spoonful of durian mousse in the centre of the plate and top with a crisp. Put a scoop, or quenelle, of sorbet on the milk crisp and place another crisp on top. Top with a tsp of whipped cream, 2 jackfruit strips and a fresh herb sprig. Blend the emulsion with a hand blender and place 2 spoonfuls of the foam on each plate. Serve immediately.

TIPS

Be careful when making the durian mousse. It's important that the mousse be as light as possible. Be sure to gently fold the cream into the durian purée and not to whisk or even mix it.

For information on simple syrups and how to make sorbet if you don't have an ice cream machine, see Techniques (page 140).

durian-chocolate caramelised filo with black rice sauce and coconut emulsion

ABOUT THE RECIPE: This durian recipe we developed at Mozaic is one of my favourites. Firstly, because it's served warm, which durian rarely is, secondly, because it's served in a crunchy filo casing that adds a texture you wouldn't usually find in a durian dish, and lastly, because the durian is combined with chocolate. Believe it or not, the combination of durian and chocolate is magical. The bitterness of the cocoa overrides the unpleasant, or let's say bitter, aftertaste of the durian, so the durian becomes perfect (at least to me). Rich and pungent at the first bite with a chocolate finish, what else could a chocolate fiend and durian lover like me want? It's the perfect combination of East and West.

PORTION: Serves 10 **DIFFICULTY LEVEL:**

INGREDIENTS

Chocolate-Durian Filos
70 ml cream
1 pinch salt
80 g milk chocolate, chopped
100 g compound chocolate, chopped
4 sheets filo pastry
70 g durian
25 g butter, melted
icing sugar, as needed

Black Rice Sauce
60 g fermented black rice
1 tsp brem (Balinese rice wine)

Emulsion
100 ml coconut milk
2–3 tbsp water
1½ tsp sugar
1 pinch salt
1 pandan leaf

Garnishes
60 thin jackfruit strips
10 fresh herb tips of your choice

METHOD

To make the ganache, bring the cream and salt to the boil. Pour it over the chocolate and stir until the chocolate has melted and the mixture is smooth. Refrigerate. Once cold, shape the ganache into round balls of approximately 2 tsp each. They should be 2 cm in diameter. Freeze.

When the ganache balls are hard on the outside, place the compound chocolate in a mixing bowl over a saucepan of simmering water. Once it has melted, remove it from the heat and allow it to cool for a few minutes, stirring continuously. Once the chocolate is lukewarm (approximately 35°C), dip the ganache balls in the chocolate so they are coated all over. Refrigerate until hard. Meanwhile, cut the filo pastry into 8 x 8 cm squares. Lay 2 squares on top of each other. Place a ball of ganache in the centre of each and top it with 1 tbsp of durian. Wrap the filo around the ganache and durian to enclose it. Refrigerate or freeze.

To make the fermented black rice sauce, blend the rice and brem until smooth. Strain and set aside.

To prepare the emulsion, place the coconut milk, water, sugar and salt in a saucepan. If the coconut milk is very thick, add a little extra water. Bring the mixture to the boil. Remove from the heat, add the pandan leaf, cover with a lid and allow it to infuse for 10 minutes. Strain and set aside.

To cook the ganache filos, preheat the oven to 180°C. Brush the filos with melted butter and dust them with icing sugar. Bake them until the centre is just warm; this should take 6–12 minutes, depending on whether they were refrigerated or frozen.

Drizzle the plates with the black rice sauce. Arrange 2 filos on each plate. Top the filos with the jackfruit. Use a hand blender to foam up the coconut milk and drop a few spoonfuls of foam on each plate. Decorate with a fresh herb sprig and serve immediately.

TIPS

When cooking, you may find the filos burst in the oven and the chocolate oozes out. There are a couple of reasons for this. Sometimes the balls of ganache are too big for the filo parcel, or the oven is not hot enough and it takes longer for the filo to crisp up and turn colour, so the chocolate overheats and oozes out.

If you can't find fermented black rice, serve these filos with a marmalade of roasted seasonal fruit and a mint julienne.

techniques

Caramel

A caramel is sugar that has melted, darkened and developed into a thick syrup. Simply add the amount of sugar in the recipe to a saucepan, and stir it over medium heat until it melts. Continue to stir and after approximately 5 minutes, the sugar will turrn deep-amber (don't allow it to go black) and caramelise. If you need to use it cold, stop it from darkening further by placing the pan in a bowl of iced water.

Chicken Stock

Chicken stock is a light yet fragrant broth that is made from chicken, vegetables and aromatics. Combine 2 kg of chicken carcasses, 1 large quartered onion, 4 carrots and 4 celery stalks, roughly chopped, the white part of 1 leek, 10 sprigs each of thyme and parsley, a bay leaf and some peppercorns in a pot, and cover with water. Bring it to the boil, then immediately turn down the heat so it is gently simmering. Simmer uncovered for 1½–2 hours, occasionally skimming any impurities off the surface. Strain the liquid and refrigerate it. Once it is cold, skim the fat off the surface. It can be used immediately or stored in a refrigerator for up to 5 days, or longer if frozen. I suggest freezing it in small amounts of around 100ml, so you can defrost as much or as little as you need.

Demi-glaçe

A demi-glaçe is a reduced beef stock that can be used as a base for many sauces. It takes a lot of effort, but the results are worth it. If you are pushed for time, demi-glaçe can be bought in a store, but it will not have the same rich flavour. Roast 10 kg of veal or beef bones until they turn dark brown. Put the roasted bones in a pot with 10 litres of water and bring it to the boil, skimming any impurities off the surface. Add a roughly-chopped, raw *mirepoix* consisting of 5 onions, 8 carrots, 1 celery stalk and 1 leek, 300 g of tomato paste, a bouquet garni and a pinch of salt. Gently simmer for 12 hours. Strain. Reduce the liquid down to 4 litres. Heat some oil in a pan and sweat 100 g chopped shallots or onions. Add a bottle of red wine and reduce it by a quarter. Add the reduced beef stock and simmer until the liquid has reduced and thickened. Please note: for the recipes in this book, the demi-glaçe should not be too thick so other flavours can be infused into it.

Foams

Foam is a wonderful alternative in dishes where a sauce would be too heavy and cloying. Depending on the ingredients, you may not be able to create a strong foam without butter or soy lecithin – the recipe will specify the ingredient needed, if any. To emulsify a liquid, simply use a hand blender to blend the liquid. Add the specified amount of soy lecithin and blend until a strong foam is created. Foams should be used immediately as most won't hold their shape for a long period of time.

Glucose and Gelatine

The liquid glucose in my sorbets is optional. It's used by chefs to stop the sorbet forming ice particles, which helps give it a better texture. The gelatine helps set the sorbet and preserve its shape longer without melting; we also add gelatine to whipped cream for the same reason. This is very useful in warm climates, such as Bali, but it wouldn't be necessary in cooler climates.

Ice Cream and Sorbet

If you don't have an ice cream machine you can make sorbet and ice cream by hand, although the result will be a little more icy. Once you have prepared the sorbet mixture, pour it into a shallow baking dish and freeze it for approximately 2 hours. As soon as the edges start to harden, remove the dish from the freezer and whisk the sorbet or ice cream to break up the ice crystals. Repeat the process twice, then allow it to freeze completely.

Kaffir Lime Salt

Kaffir lime salt (as well as other types of flavoured salts) allows you to infuse a lot of extra flavour into your meat and fish dishes, and it can also be used in dressings and other condiments. Simply mix 4 tbsp of sea salt and 1 tbsp of finely grated kaffir lime zest by hand until the salt turns green. Place the salt it in a preheated160°C oven for 3 minutes to dry out the salt. Once it has dried (it should still be bright green), allow it to cool to room temperature. It can be stored in an airtight container for up to 1 week. Its flavour will remain during that time, but the bright green colour will fade after 24 hours.

Low Oven Temperatures

Many of my recipes call for very low oven temperatures. Some home ovens may not have a temperature control for under 100°C. If that is the case, there are a number of things you can do to create the right cooking environment. Set the oven temperature to the minimum and use an oven thermometer to check the heat. Alternatively, you can try leaving the oven door slightly ajar while cooking. If that doesn't work and you are cooking meat, you can preheat your oven to 150–200°C, depending on the specified temperature, put the meat in and turn the oven off for the remainder of the cooking time.

Roasted Bell Peppers

Roasting peppers can give them a sweet flavour that is great in salads, pastas and many other dishes. Preheat the oven to 200–220°C. Cut the bell peppers in half and remove the stem, seeds and white membranes. Place them in a bowl with olive oil, salt and pepper, and mix well. Place the bell pepper halves on an oven tray and roast them until they are cooked; they should be very soft to the touch. Remove them from the oven and place them in a sealed plastic bag or bowl covered with cling film for 5 minutes to steam. Remove them from the bag or bowl, and peel or rub the skin to remove it. To store the peppers, you can cover them in olive oil and store in the fridge for up to 1 week.

Roasted Garlic

It is simple to roast garlic, after which, its sweeter, more subtle flavours really come to the fore. Place whole, unpeeled heads of garlic in a 180–200°C oven and roast them until they are soft. Cool to room temperature then squeeze or pull the cloves out of their skins with your hands. Confied garlic is somewhat similar in taste. To make it, simply peel the garlic, submerge it in salad or olive oil and cook it over very low heat until it is soft. Roasted garlic is a good condiment for a wide variety of dishes and can be stored (strained from its oil) in the refrigerator for up to 1 week.

Simple Syrup

A simple syrup is a mixture of water and sugar that is based on various ratios of these two ingredients. Because of this, the water is always weighed and not measured by volume. In this book, I make a simple syrup using a ratio of 1:1, however, other syrups can be made using different ratios. For example, a ratio of 3 parts water to 1 part sugar is used as a glaze for cakes and other baked goods, or for drinks. To make a simple syrup, add the ratio of water and sugar specified in the recipe to a saucepan. Bring the water to the boil, stirring to completely dissolve the sugar, then remove it from the heat. It is now ready for use.

Zesting Citrus Fruit

Zest (the outermost, colourful layer) is a great addition to dishes due to the flavour contained in the skin. Depending on the preparation, you can remove the zest in a number of ways. For grated zest, I recommend using a fine microplane grater, as it grates only the zest and none of the bitter white pith. For peeled zest, I use either a sharp knife or vegetable peeler to cut off wide strips. For citrus peel (both zest and white pith), I recommend cutting the skin off with a serrated knife.

glossary

Balinese sea salt: This salt is produced by evaporating sea water in long wooden troughs on beaches along the east coast of Bali. It is available as a damp, coarse, rich-tasting salt in farmers' markets. The most distinctive salt produced in Bali is the pyramid-shaped natural crystal salt that is good enough to eat with a small spoon. Balinese sea salt is called *garam* in Indonesia and *tasik* in Balinese. It can be substituted with any good quality sea salt.

Candlenut (*Aleurites moluccana*, *Euphorbiaceae*): A round, waxy, pale-yellow nut with a high oil content and bitter flavour. Used as a thickening agent in Southeast Asian cooking, where it is ground to a paste, or slivers that are dry roasted and added to stews. Raw candlenut may contain toxins. Candlenut is called *kemiri* in Indonesian and *tingkih* in Balinese. Macadamia nuts may work as a substitute in some recipes.

Cocoa (*Theobroma cacao*, *Malvaceae*): Also known as cacao. The cocoa pod is an oval fruit containing 20–60 seeds or "beans" composed of up to 50% cocoa butter, the source of chocolate. The beans are surrounded by a white membrane that tastes wonderful. The roasted beans can be used in cooking, and add a powerful cocoa flavour and a crunchy texture to dishes. Roasted and crushed beans are sold as chocolate nibs (*grué* in French). Cocoa is called *kakao* in Indonesian and *coklat* in Balinese. You can substitute unsweetened chocolate for cocoa or cocoa beans in some recipes.

Cumin leaf (*Coleus amboinicus Lour* or *Coleus aromaticus Benth.*, *Labiatae*): Cumin leaf is the English translation of the Indonesian *daun jinten*, not the leaf of the cumin plant that produces the familiar cumin seeds. It is a plant with soft, fleshy pale green leaves and a tall stalk of tiny purple flowers. It has a bright fragrant aroma with nuances of oregano, camphor and mint. Cumin leaf is called *don dèlem* in Balinese. Cumin leaf is also known as broadleaf thyme, Spanish thyme, Cuban oregano, Indian borage, Indian mint and Mexican mint. No substitute.

Genjer leaf (*Limnocharis flava* (L.) *Buchenau 1868*, *Limnocharitaceae*): Genjer leaf is an aquatic plant with leaves shaped like a pointed spoon. It grows as a weed in rice fields, and is used as a vegetable in Java and other parts of Indonesia. The leaf has an interesting texture and an iodine aroma that makes it ideal in steaming fish. It is called *don genjer* in Balinese and is also known as yellow burrhead and yellow velvetleaf. No substitute.

Kenari nut (also Java almond, pili nut) (*Canarium indicum*, *Burseraceae*): As the English name implies, the kenari nut is similar in taste to the almond, but is flatter, oval and pale cream-coloured. Its 70% oil content is the highest of any nut. In Indonesia, it is used as a thickener. In east Indonesia, they are eaten raw when young as a source of protein and oil. Substitute them with almonds.

Konnyaku jelly powder: A powder found in Asian grocery stores that is used to make gelatinous desserts and snacks. It is made from carrageenan seaweed and konjac root powders. At Mozaic, it is used to turn liquids into jellies that can be shaped and served warm without melting.

Kuweni mango (*Mangifera odorata*, *Anacardiaceae*): An unusual mango that is native to Southeast Asia. The tree is named after the strong, fragrant, resinous smell of its sap. The oval fruit is green when ripe. The flesh is white, very sweet and has a pungent taste. This fruit should be eaten only when fully ripe; the sap of the unripe fruit is poisonous. It is called *wani* in Indonesian and is also known as kuini mango. No substitute.

Laksa leaf (*Persicaria odorata*, *Polygonaceae*): A herb with tender blade-like leaves and a peppery, mint-like flavour with traces of citrus, coriander and pine. These leaves are used only in the northern parts of Indonesia, where the leaf grows. The chopped leaves are added as an aromatic herb in dishes like heavy curries. The laksa leaf is called *daun laksa* in Indonesian and *daun kesom* in Malay. It is also known as Vietnamese coriander, Vietnamese mint and hot mint. No substitute.

Lombok chilli (*Capsicum annuum L. var. grossum* (*L.*) *Sendt.*): A large green or red, mild chilli that originated in Lombok, an island east of Bali. This chilli is commonly used in all Indonesian cuisine – not for its heat, but for the aroma that it brings to a dish. Heat is then added with other spicier chillies. Lombok chilli is called *cabe Lombok* in Indonesian and *tabia gede* in Balinese. It can be substituted with any fresh mild chilli.

Mamey sapote (*Pouteria sapota*, *Sapotaceae*): A melon native to Central America, with orange flesh and a flavour similar to sweet potato or pumpkin, with traces of chocolate and almond. No substitute.

Pandan leaf (*Pandanus amaryllifolius*, *Pandanaceae*): The leaf of the versatile pandanus plant has a gentle, fragrant vanilla-like aroma, and is used for flavouring in Southeast Asian cooking in both sweet and savoury dishes. It must be cooked to release its full flavour. It is called *daun pandan* in Indonesian. No substitute.

Rosewater apple (*Syzygium aqueum Alst.* or *Eugenia aquea Burm. f.*, *Myrtacea*): A small, crisp, slightly sweet but often sour, watery fruit whose colour ranges from white to bright pink (with some varieties in green, brown and red). It is called *jambu air* in Indonesian. No substitute.

Salam leaf (*Eugenia polyantha Wight.*, *Syzygium polyanthum* (Wight) *Waplers*, *Myrtaceae*): An aromatic, astringent leaf used in most Indonesian fish, meat and vegetable dishes. When cooked, the leaf has a pleasant aroma. It is not used on its own, but complements other spices. It is called *daun/don salam* in Indonesian/Balinese. Salam leaves are available dry and can be substituted with bay leaves, though their aroma is completely different.

Sapodilla (*Manilkara zapota*, *Sapotaceae*): A round, brown-skinned fruit 5–10cm wide, native to Central America and Southeast Asia. The flesh is yellow to red to brown with a pear-like texture and is very sweet, with a flavour likened to brown sugar and root beer. It is called *sawo* in Indonesian, *saba* in Balinese and *buah chiku* in Malay. No substitute.

Shrimp paste: A raw, pungent, salty, strong smelling paste made of fermented shrimp that is sun-dried and cut into blocks. Dry roast in a pan before use. It is called *terasi* in Indonesian, *belacan* in Malay and *seraa* in Balinese. No substitute.

Tenggulun berries: These grow in the wild in the northern forests of Bali or Lombok. The leaves of the tenggulun tree are sometimes used to infuse things like tea. When cooked, they have a complex aroma made of many spices, such as vanilla, clove, star anise, cinnamon and others. No substitute.

Turmeric leaves: The leaf of the turmeric plant (*Curcuma longa Linn.*, *Zingiberaceae*) has the subtle aroma of turmeric. It's used in Balinese cooking in coconut-based vegetable dishes (*sayur roroban*) and steamed or grilled leaf-wrapped dishes (*pepèsan*). Imparts no colour. Called *daun/don kunyit* in Indonesian/Balinese. No substitute.

There are many more amazing ingredients I wish to share with you, but to include them all would take a whole book in itself. Nonetheless, Bali has a whole host of unique ingredients and I urge you to seek them out.

index

photo credits

Unless listed below, all pictures are provided courtesy of Philippe Heurtault (except p.20, p.21, p.25 (no.5)
Jayesh Madhoo, p.14 (centre left), p.22 (no.8) and p.23 (no.12)
Tim De Boeck/istock Photos, p.14 (bottom left)
Carlina Teteris/Getty Images, p.14 (top right)
Joakim Leroy/istock Photos, p.19 (centre right)
Albrecht G. Schaefer/Corbis, p.19 (bottom right)
Richard Watson, p.24 (no.1 and no.8)

SECURITY
SECURITY
mozaic
SECURITY
SATPAM
mozaic
mozaic